Working Words in **Spelling**

REVISED EDITION

W9-BHY-144

Word-finder

A Quick Spelling Reference for Student Writers

Moore
Woodruff
Forest
Talbot
Talbot
Johnson
DiGiammarino

D.C. Heath and Company
HEATH Lexington, Massachusetts / Toronto, Ontario

Heath Wordfinder

George Moore
G. Willard Woodruff
Robert Forest

Richard Talbot
Ann Talbot
Donald Johnson

Frank DiGiammarino

Choosing the Best Word Form

The Heath Wordfinder contains over four thousand base words and over thirteen thousand other word forms. It is organized to help you quickly and easily find the form of the word that is the best one to use in your everyday writing. The Wordfinder is organized so that the entry form is usually the base form. Following this are other forms of each entry word with various endings, such as **–s, –ed, –ing, –er, –est, –ly, –es, –ment,** and **–tion.**

These endings or suffixes are important to us as writers. They help us to use the correct tense or part of speech. They are, however, more difficult to spell than the base words from which they originated. To help you with this difficulty, the Wordfinder shows most of the endings so you can be sure of their correct spellings when you use them in your everyday writing.

Using your Heath Wordfinder daily will help you become a more accurate and powerful speller.

Published simultaneously in Canada

Printed in the United States of America

International Standard Book Number: 0-669-31422-6

2 3 4 5 6 7 8 9 10 -BA- 99 98 97 96 95 94

A

abandon abandons, abandoned, abandoning, abandonment

able   abler, ablest, ability, abilities

about

above

absent absence, absences, absentee, absenteeism, absently

absolute absolutely, absoluteness

abstract   abstracts, abstractly, abstractness

abundant abundantly, abundance, abundancy

accent accents, accented, accenting

accept accepts, accepted, accepting, acceptable, acceptably, acceptance, acceptability

accident   accidents, accidental, accidentally

accommodate accommodates, accommodated, accommodating, accommodatingly, accommodative, accommodation, accommodator, accommodators

accompany accompanies, accompanied, accompanying, accompaniment, accompanist, accompanists

accomplish   accomplishes, accomplished, accomplishing, accomplishable, accomplishment, accomplishments

accord accords, accorded, according, accordingly, accordance

1

account accounts, accounted, accounting, accountable, accountant, accountants

accurate accurately, accuracy, accurateness

accuse accuses, accused, accusing, accusingly, accuser, accusation, accusations

accustom accustoms, accustomed

ache aches, ached, aching

achieve achieves, achieved, achieving, achievable, achievement, achievements, achiever, achievers

acid acids, acidic, acidly, acidity, acidness

acknowledge acknowledges, acknowledged, acknowledging, acknowledgeable, acknowledgment, acknowledgments

acquaint acquaints, acquainted, acquainting, acquaintance, acquaintances

acquire acquires, acquired, acquiring

acre acres, acreage

across

act acts, acted, acting, action, actions, actor, actors, actress, actresses

active actively, activate, activates, activated, activating, activeness, activism, activist, activity, activities

actual actually, actualize, actualized, actualizes, actualizing, actuality, actualization, actualizations

acute acutely, acuteness

adapt adapts, adapted, adapting, adaptive, adaptable, adapter, adapters, adaptation, adaptations

add adds, added, adding, addend, addendum, adder, addition, additions, additional, additionally, additive, additives

address addresses, addressed, addressing

adequate adequately, adequacy, adequateness

adjourn adjourns, adjourned, adjourning, adjournment, adjournments

adjust adjusts, adjusted, adjusting, adjustable, adjustment, adjuster, adjusters

administer administers, administered, administering, administrate, administrative, administration, administrations, administrator, administrators

admire admires, admired, admiring, admirable, admirably, admiringly, admirability, admiration, admirer, admirers

admit admits, admitted, admitting, admittedly, admittance, admission, admissions

adopt adopts, adopted, adopting, adoptable, adopter, adoption, adoptions

advance advances, advanced, advancing, advancer, advancement, advancements

advantage advantages, advantageous, advantageously

adventure adventures, adventured, adventuring, adventurer, adventurers, adventurous, adventurously, adventuresome

advertise advertises, advertised, advertising, advertisement, advertisements, advertiser, advertisers

advise advises, advised, advising, advice, adviser, advisers

affair affairs

affect affects, affected, affecting, affectionate, affectionately, affectation, affection, affections

afford affords, afforded, affording, affordable, affordably

afraid

after

afternoon afternoons

afterward afterwards

again

against

age ages, aged, aging

agent agents, agency, agencies

ago

agree agrees, agreed, agreeing, agreeable, agreeably, agreeableness, agreement, agreements, agreeability

agriculture agricultural, agriculturally

ahead

aid   aids, aided, aiding

aim   aims, aimed, aiming, aimless, aimlessly, aimlessness

air   airs, aired, airing, airy

airport   airports

aisle   aisles

alarm   alarms, alarmed, alarming, alarmingly

alike   alikeness

alive

all

alley   alleys

allow   allows, allowed, allowing, allowable, allowably, allowance, allowances

all right

almost

alone

along

already

also

alter   alters, altered, altering, alteration, alterations

although

altogether

always

ambassador   ambassadors, ambassadorial, ambassadorship, ambassadorships

ambition   ambitions, ambitionless, ambitious, ambitiously

ambulate   ambulates, ambulated, ambulating, ambulation, ambulatory

ambulance   ambulances

amend   amends, amended, amending, amendable, amendment, amendments

America   Americas, American, Americans, Americanism

ammunition   ammunitions

among   amongst

amount   amounts, amounted, amounting

ample   amply, ampleness

amuse   amuses, amused, amusing, amusingly, amusable, amusement, amusements

an

analyze   analyzes, analyzed, analyzing, analytic, analytical, analytically, analysis, analyses, analyst

ancestor   ancestors, ancestral, ancestry, ancestries

anchor   anchors, anchored, anchoring, anchorage, anchorages

ancient   ancients, ancientness

and

anger   angers, angered, angering, angry, angrier, angriest, angrily

angle   angles, angled, angling

animal animals

animate animates, animated, animating, animation, animator, animators

ankle ankles

anniversary anniversaries

announce announces, announced, announcing, announcement, announcements, announcer, announcers

annual annuals, annually

another

answer answers, answered, answering

ant ants

anticipate anticipates, anticipated, anticipating, anticipatory, anticipation

anxiety anxieties, anxious, anxiously, anxiousness

any anybody, anyhow, anyone, anything, anyway, anywhere

apartment apartments

apiece

apology apologies, apologize, apologizes, apologized, apologizing

apparent apparently, apparentness

appeal appeals, appealed, appealing, appealingly

appear appears, appeared, appearing, appearance, appearances

appetite appetites, appetize, appetizer, appetizers

apple apples

appliance appliances

apply applies, applied, applying, applicable, applicant, applicants, application, applications, applicator, applicators

appoint appoints, appointed, appointing, appointment, appointments

appreciate appreciates, appreciated, appreciating, appreciable, appreciative, appreciably, appreciation, appreciations

approach approaches, approached, approaching, approachable

approve approves, approved, approving, approvingly, approval, approvals

approximate approximates, approximated, approximating, approximately, approximation, approximations

April Apr.

apron aprons, aproned

are aren't

area areas

argue argues, argued, arguing, argument, arguments, argumentative

arithmetic arithmetical

arm arms

army armies

armor armors, armored, armory

around

arrange   arranges, arranged, arranging, arranger, arrangement, arrangements

arrest   arrests, arrested, arresting, arrester, arresters

arrive   arrives, arrived, arriving, arrival, arrivals

arrow   arrows

art   arts, artist, artists, artistic, artistically, artistry

article   articles

artificial   artificially, artificialness

as

ash   ashes, ashy

aside   asides

ask   asks, asked, asking

asleep

assemble   assembles, assembled, assembling, assemblage, assembly, assemblies, assembler, assemblers

assign   assigns, assigned, assigning, assignable, assigner, assignment, assignments

assist   assists, assisted, assisting, assistance, assistant, assistants

associate   associates, associated, associating, association, associations

assort   assorts, assorted, assorting, assortment, assortments

assume   assumes, assumed, assuming, assumable, assumer, assumption, assumptions

assure   assures, assured, assuring, assuredly, assurance, assurances, assurer, assurers

astonish   astonishes, astonished, astonishing, astonishingly, astonishment

astronaut   astronauts, astronautic, astronautics, astronautical

at

athlete   athletes, athletic, athletically, athletics

atmosphere   atmospheres, atmospheric, atmospherical, atmospherically

attach   attaches, attached, attaching, attachable, attachment, attachments

attack   attacks, attacked, attacking, attacker, attackers

attain   attains, attained, attaining, attainable, attainment

attempt   attempts, attempted, attempting

attend   attends, attended, attending, attendance, attentive, attentively, attentiveness, attendant, attendants

attention   attentions

attic   attics

attitude   attitudes

attorney   attorneys

attract attracts, attracted, attracting, attractive, attractively, attractiveness, attraction, attractions

auction auctions, auctioned, auctioning, auctioneer, auctioneers

audience audiences

auditorium auditoriums

August Aug.

aunt aunts

author authors, authored, authoring

authority authorities, authorize, authorization, authoritarian, authoritative

automobile automobiles, auto

automate automates, automated, automating

automatic automation

autumn autumns

avail avails, availed, availing, available, availably, availableness, availability

avenue avenues, Ave.

average averages, averaged, averaging

aviation aviator, aviators

avoid avoids, avoided, avoiding, avoidable, avoidably, avoidance

await awaits, awaited, awaiting

awake awakes, awaked, awoke, awaking, awaken, awakens

aware awareness

away

away

awful   awfully, awfulness

awkward   awkwardly, awkwardness

ax   axes, axed, axing

B

baby   babies, babied, babying, babyish

back   backs, backward, backwards

backfire   backfires, backfired, backfiring, backfirings

bacteria   bacterium

bad   badly, badness

badge   badges

bait   baits, baited, baiting

bake   bakes, baked, baking, baker, bakers, bakery, bakeries

balance   balances, balanced, balancing, balancer

ball   balls

ballet   ballets, ballerina, ballerinas

balloon   balloons, ballooned, ballooning

ballot   ballots, balloted, balloting

banana   bananas

band   bands

bang   bangs, banged, banging

banister   banisters

bank   banks, banked, banking, banker, bankers

bankrupt   bankruptcy, bankruptcies, bankrupts, bankrupting

banner   banners

banquet   banquets, banqueted, banqueting

13

barbecue barbecues, barbecued, barbecuing

bare bares, bared, baring, barer, barest, barely, bareness

bargain bargains, bargained, bargaining, bargainer, bargainers

baritone baritones

bark barks, barked, barking

barn barns

barrel barrels, barreled, barreling, barrelful, barrelfuls

base bases, based, basing, basis, basic, basically

baseball baseballs

basement basements

basket baskets

basketball basketballs

bat bats

bath baths, bathing, bathed, bathe, bathes, bather, bathers

battery batteries

battle battles, battled, battling, battler, battlers

bazaar bazaars

be am, is, was, were, been, being

beach beaches

bead beads, beaded, beading

beam beams, beamed, beaming

bean beans

bear bears, bore, borne, bearing, bearable, bearably, bearer, bearers

beast beasts, beastly

beat beats, beating, beaten, beater, beaters

beautiful beautifully, beauty, beautify, beautified, beautifying, beautification

because

become becomes, becoming, became

bed beds

bedroom bedrooms

bedtime bedtimes

bee bees

beef beefy

before

beg begs, begged, begging, beggar, beggars

begin begins, began, begun, beginning, beginner, beginners

behave behaves, behaved, behaving, behavior, behaviors, behavioral, behaviorally

behind

believe believes, believed, believing, believable, believably, believability, belief, beliefs

bell bells

belong belongs, belonged, belonging, belongings

below

belt   belts, belted

bench   benches

bend   bends, bent, bending, bendable

beneath

benefit   benefits, benefited, benefiting,
    beneficial, beneficiary, beneficiaries

berry   berries

beside

best   better

bestow   bestows, bestowed, bestowing,
    bestowal

bet   bets, betted, betting, bettor, bettors

betray   betrays, betrayed, betraying,
    betrayer, betrayal

between

bewilder   bewilders, bewildered,
    bewildering, bewilderingly,
    bewilderment, bewilderments

beyond

bicycle   bicycles, bicycled, bicycling,
    bicycler, bicyclist, bicyclists

bid   bids, bidder, bidding

big   bigger, biggest

bike   bikes, biked, biking

bill   bills, billed, billing

bind   binds, binder, binding

bird   birds

16

birth   births

birthday   birthdays

biscuit   biscuits

bite   bites, biting, bit, bitten, biter, biters

bitter   bitterly, bitterness

black   blacker, blackest

blade   blades

blame   blames, blamed, blaming, blameless

blanket   blankets, blanketed, blanketing

blast   blasts, blasted, blasting

blaze   blazes, blazed, blazing

blimp   blimps

blind   blinds, blinded, blinding, blindly, blindness

blizzard   blizzards

block   blocks, blocked, blocking, blocker, blockers

blood   bleed, bleeds, bleeding, bled, bloody, bloodier, bloodiest, bloodiness

bloom   blooms, bloomed, blooming, bloomer, bloomers

blossom   blossoms, blossomed, blossoming, blossomless

blouse   blouses

blow   blows, blew, blown, blowing, blower, blowers

blue   bluer, bluest

bluff   bluffs, bluffed, bluffing, bluffer, bluffers

board   boards, boarded, boarding, boarder

boat   boats, boating

body   bodies, bodily

boil   boils, boiled, boiling, boiler, boilers

bond   bonds, bonded, bonding, bondage

book   books

bookkeeping   bookkeeper, bookkeepers

boot   boots

border   borders, bordered, bordering

bore   bores, bored, boring, boredom

born

borrow   borrows, borrowed, borrowing, borrower, borrowers

both

bother   bothers, bothered, bothering

bottom   bottoms, bottomless

bough   boughs

boulevard   boulevards

bound   bounds, bounded, bounding, boundless, boundary, boundaries

bouquet   bouquets

bow   bows, bowed, bowing

bowl   bowls, bowled, bowling, bowler, bowlers

box   boxed, boxing, boxer, boxers

boy boys

bracelet bracelets

braid braids, braided, braiding

brain brains, brainy, brainier, brainiest, brainless

brake brakes, braked, braking

branch branches, branched, branching

brass brasses, brassy

brave braver, bravest, braves, braved, braving, bravely, braveness, bravery

bread breads

break breaks, broke, broken, breaking, breakable, breaker, breakers

breakfast breakfasts, breakfasted, breakfasting

breath breaths, breather, breathless, breathlessly, breathlessness, breathe, breathes, breathed, breathing, breathable

briar briars

brick bricks, bricked, bricking

bridge bridges, bridged, bridging

brief briefer, briefest, briefs, briefed, briefing, briefly, briefness

bright brighter, brightest, brighten, brightly, brightness

brilliance brilliant, brilliantly

bring brings, brought, bringing

broad   broader, broadest, broaden, broadens, broadened, broadening, broadly, broadness

brook   brooks

brother   brothers

brown   browner, brownest

browse   browses, browsed, browsing, browser, browsers

bruise   bruises, bruised, bruising

brush   brushes, brushed, brushing

bucket   buckets

bud   buds, budded, budding

budget   budgets, budgeted, budgeting, budgetary

bug   bugs

build   builds, built, building, buildings, builder, builders

bull   bulls, bully, bullies, bullied, bullying

bulletin   bulletins

bullpen   bullpens

bump   bumps, bumped, bumping, bumper, bumpers, bumpy

bundle   bundles, bundled, bundling, bundler, bundlers

bunny   bunnies

burden   burdens, burdened, burdening, burdensome

burglar   burglars, burglary, burglarize, burglarizes, burglarized

bureau   bureaus

bureaucrat   bureaucratic,
   bureaucratically, bureaucracy

burlap

burn   burns, burned, burnt, burning,
   burner, burners

burst   bursts, burst, bursting

bury   buries, buried, burying, burial

bus   buses

bush   bushes, bushy

bushel   bushels, busheled, busheling

bustle   bustles, bustled, bustling

busy   busies, busied, busying, busier,
   busiest, busyness, business, businesses

but

butter   butters, buttered, buttering

button   buttons, buttoned, buttoning

buy   buys, bought, buying, buyer, buyers

by

by-product   by-products

C

cabbage cabbages

cabin cabins

cabinet cabinets

cable cables, cabled

cafeteria cafeterias, cafe, cafes

cage cages

cake cakes

calamity calamities, calamitous, calamitously

calculate calculates, calculated, calculating, calculation, calculations, calculator, calculators

calendar calendars

caliber calibers, calibrate, calibrates, calibrated, calibrating, calibration, calibrator

calf calves

call calls, called, calling, caller, callers

calm calms, calmed, calming, calmer, calmest, calmly, calmness

camel camels

camp camps, camped, camping, camper, campers

campaign campaigns, campaigned, campaigning, campaigner, campaigners

campus campuses

can cannot, can't, could

canal canals

cancel cancels, cancelled, cancelling, cancellation, cancellations

candidate candidates, candidacy, candidacies

candle candles

candy candies

cane canes

canister canisters

canoe canoes, canoed, canoeing

canvas canvases

canvass canvasses, canvassed, canvassing, canvasser, canvassers

canyon canyons

cap caps

capable capably, capableness, capability, capabilities

capacity capacities

cape capes

capital capitals, capitalize, capitalizes, capitalized, capitalizing, capitalization, capitalist, capitalists

capitol capitols

captain captains, captained, captaining

capture captures, captured, capturing, captive, captives, captivity, captor, captors

car cars

carbon carbons

card

card cards

care cares, cared, caring, careful,
  carefully, carefulness

career careers

careless carelessly, carelessness

carload carloads

carnival carnivals

carpet carpets, carpeted, carpeting

carriage carriages

carry carries, carried, carrying, carrier,
  carriers

cart carts

case cases, cased, casing, casings

cash cashes, cashed, cashing, cashier,
  cashiers

cassette cassettes

castaway castaways

castle castles

cat cats, catty

catalog catalogs, cataloged, cataloging,
  cataloger, catalogers

catch catches, caught, catching, catcher,
  catchers

category categories, categorize,
  categorizes, categorized, categorizing,
  categoric, categorical, categorically,
  categorization, categorizations

cattle

cause causes, caused, causing, causable

caution cautions, cautioned, cautioning, cautionary, cautious, cautiously, cautiousness

cease ceases, ceased, ceasing, ceaseless, ceaselessly

cedar cedars

ceiling ceilings

celebrate celebrates, celebrated, celebrating, celebrant, celebration, celebrations

celebrity celebrities

cellar cellars

cement cements, cemented, cementing

cemetery cemeteries

census censuses

cent cents

center centers, centered, centering, central, centralize, centralizes, centralized, centralizing

centimeter centimeters

century centuries

cereal cereals

ceremony ceremonies, ceremonial

certain certainly, certainty

certify certifies, certified, certifying, certifiable, certifiably, certificate, certificates, certification, certifications

chain chains, chained, chaining

chair   chairs

chairperson   chairpersons

chalk   chalks, chalked, chalking, chalky

challenge   challenges, challenged,
      challenging, challengeable, challenger,
      challengers

chamber   chambers, chambered

champion   champions, championed,
      championing, championship,
      championships

chance   chances, chanced, chancing

change   changes, changed, changing,
      changeable, changeably, changeless,
      changer, changers

channel   channels, channeled, channeling

chapter   chapters

character   characters, characteristic,
      characteristics, characteristically,
      characterize, characterization,
      characterizations

charge   charges, charged, charging,
      chargeable, charger

charity   charities, charitable, charitably,
      charitableness

charm   charms, charmed, charming,
      charmer, charmingly

chart   charts, charted, charting

chase   chases, chased, chasing, chaser,
      chasers

chatter chatters, chattered, chattering, chatterer, chatterers

cheap cheaper, cheapest, cheapen, cheapens, cheapened, cheaply, cheapness

cheat cheats, cheated, cheating, cheater, cheaters

check checks, checked, checking, checker, checkers

cheer cheers, cheered, cheering, cheery, cheerier, cheeriest, cheeriness

cheerful cheerfully

cheese cheeses, cheesy

chemistry chemistries, chemical, chemicals, chemically, chemist, chemists

cherish cherishes, cherished, cherishing

cherry cherries

chest chests

chew chews, chewed, chewing, chewy, chewier, chewiest

chicken chickens

chief chiefs, chiefly, chieftain, chieftains

child children, childish, childlike, childhood, childhoods

chill chills, chilled, chilling, chilly

chimney chimneys

chocolate chocolates, chocolaty

choir choirs

choice choices, choicer, choicest

choose　chooses, chose, choosing, chosen, choosy, chooser, choosier, choosiest, choosiness

chop　chops, chopped, chopping, chopper

chorus　choruses, chorused, chorusing, choral

circle　circles, circled, circling, circular

circuit　circuits, circuited, circuiting, circuitous, circuitously, circuitry, circuitries

circulate　circulates, circulated, circulating, circulation, circulator, circulatory

circumference　circumferential

circumstance　circumstances, circumstanced, circumstantial, circumstantially

circus　circuses

citizen　citizens, citizenry, citizenship

city　cities

civil　civilly, civilian, civilians, civilize, civilizes, civilized, civilizing, civilization, civilizations

claim　claims, claimed, claiming, claimable, claimant, claimants

clammy　clammier, clammiest, clamminess

clamor　clamors, clamored, clamoring, clamorous, clamorously

clap　claps, clapped, clapping

class   classes, classed, classical, classifier,
classify, classifies, classified,
classifying, classification, classifications

clay

clean   cleans, cleaned, cleaning, cleaner,
cleaners, cleanest

clear   clearer, clearest, clearly, clears,
cleared, clearing, clearness, clarity

clerk   clerks, clerked, clerking, clerical

clever   cleverer, cleverest, cleverly,
cleverness

cliff   cliffs

climate   climates, climatic

climax   climaxes, climaxed, climaxing,
climactic

climb   climbs, climbed, climbing, climber,
climbers

clock   clocks

close   closes, closed, closing, closer, closest,
closely, closeness

closet   closets

cloth   cloths, clothe, clothes, clothed,
clothing

cloud   clouds, clouded, clouding, cloudy,
cloudiness

clown   clowns, clowned, clowning, clownish

club   clubs, clubbed, clubbing

cluster   clusters, clustered, clustering

coach   coaches, coached, coaching

coal   coals

coarse   coarser, coarsest, coarsen, coarsened, coarsely, coarseness

coast   coasts, coasted, coasting, coastal, coaster, coasters

coat   coats

cocoa

cocoon   cocoons

coin   coins, coined, coining, coinage, coinages

coincide   coincides, coincided, coinciding, coincident, coincidental, coincidently, coincidentally, coincidence, coincidences

cold   colder, coldest, colds

collar   collars, collared, collaring

collect   collects, collected, collecting, collectable, collector, collectors, collection, collections

college   colleges, collegiate, collegian, collegians

colonel   colonels

colony   colonies, colonize, colonizes, colonized, colonizing, colonization, colonial, colonially, colonialism, colonist, colonists

color   colors, colored, coloring, colorful, colorfully

colossal   colossally, colossus

colt   colts

column columns, columned, columnist, columnists

comb combs, combed, combing

combine combines, combined, combining, combination, combinations

combust combusts, combusted, combusting, combustible, combustion

come comes, came, coming

comet comets

comfort comforts, comforted, comforting, comfortable, comfortably, comfortableness, comforter, comforters

command commands, commanded, commanding, commander, commandment, commandments

commence commences, commenced, commencing, commencement, commencements

commend commends, commended, commending, commendable, commendably, commendation, commendations

comment comments, commented, commenting, commentator, commentators

commerce commercial, commercials, commercially, commercialism, commercialization, commercializations

commission commissions, commissioned, commissioning, commissioner, commissioners

commit commits, committed, committing, committedly, commitment, commitments, committal

committee committees

common commoner, commonest, commonly, commonness

communicate communicates, communicated, communicating, communication, communications, communicator, communicators

community communities

commute commutes, commuted, commuting, commuter, commuters

companion companions, companionable, companionship, companionships

company companies

compare compares, compared, comparing, comparable, comparably, comparative, comparatively, comparison, comparisons

compass compasses

compel compels, compelled, compelling, compellingly

compensate compensates, compensated, compensating, compensation, compensative, compensatory, compensator, compensators

compete competes, competed, competing, competitive, competitively, competition, competitions, competitor, competitors, competitiveness

competent competently, competence, competency, competencies

complain complains, complained, complaining, complainant, complainer, complainers

complement complements, complemented, complementing, complementary

complete completes, completed, completing, completely, completeness, completion, completions

complex complexes, complexly, complexity, complexities

compliment compliments, complimented, complimenting, complimentary

comply complies, complied, complying, compliant, compliantly, compliance

compose composes, composed, composing, composite, composer, composition, compositions

comprehend comprehends, comprehended, comprehending, comprehensible, comprehension, comprehensive, comprehensiveness

compromise compromises, compromised, compromising, compromisingly, compromiser, compromisers

compute computes, computed, computing, computerize, computer, computers

conceal conceals, concealed, concealing, concealable, concealment

conceit conceits, conceited, conceiting, conceitedly, conceitedness

concern concerns, concerned, concerning

concert concerts, concerto, concertos

conclude concludes, concluded, concluding, conclusive, conclusively, conclusion, conclusions, conclusiveness

concrete   concretes, concretely, concreteness

condemn   condemns, condemned, condemning, condemnable, condemnation

condition   conditions, conditioned, conditioning, conditional, conditionally, conditioner, conditioners

conduct   conducts, conducted, conducting, conductible, conductive, conductibility, conductivity, conduction, conductor, conductors

confer   confers, conferred, conferring, conference, conferences

confide   confides, confided, confiding, confident, confidently, confidential, confidentially, confidant, confidants, confidence, confidences, confidentiality

confine   confines, confined, confining, confinement, confinements

confirm   confirms, confirmed, confirming, confirmation, confirmations

conflict   conflicts, conflicted, conflicting

confuse   confuses, confused, confusing, confusingly, confusedly, confusion, confusions

congratulate   congratulates, congratulated, congratulating, congratulatory, congratulation, congratulations

congress   congresses, congressional

connect   connects, connected, connecting, connective, connector, connectors, connection, connections

conquer conquers, conquered, conquering, conqueror, conquerors

conscience consciences, conscientious, conscientiously

conscious consciously, consciousness

consent consents, consented, consenting

consequent consequently, consequential, consequentially, consequence, consequences

consider considers, considered, considering, consideration, considerations, considerable, considerably, considerate, considerately

consist consists, consisted, consisting, consistent, consistently, consistence, consistency, consistencies

conspicuous conspicuously, conspicuousness

constant constants, constantly, constancy

constitute constitutes, constituted, constituting, constitution, constitutions, constitutional, constitutionally

construct constructs, constructed, constructing, construction, constructions, constructive, constructively

consult consults, consulted, consulting, consultation, consultations, consultant, consultants

consume consumes, consumed, consuming, consumable, consumption, consumer, consumers

contact contacts, contacted, contacting

contain contains, contained, containing, containable, containment, container, containers

contemplate contemplates, contemplated, contemplating

contemporary contemporaries

content contents, contented, contentedly, contentment, contentments

contest contests, contestant, contestants

continent continents, continental

continue continues, continued, continuing, continual, continually, continuous, continuously, continuance, continuation, continuations

contract contracts, contracted, contracting, contraction, contractions, contractor, contractors

contradict contradicts, contradicted, contradicting, contradictable, contradictory, contradiction, contradictions

contrary contrarily, contrariness

contrast contrasts, contrasted, contrasting, contrastable

contribute contributes, contributed, contributing, contributor, contributors, contribution, contributions

control controls, controlled, controlling, controllable, controller, controllers

controversy controversies, controversial, controversially

convene convenes, convened, convening

convenience conveniences, convenient, conveniently

convention conventions

converse converses, conversed, conversing, conversation, conversations, conversational, conversationalist, conversely

convey conveys, conveyed, conveying, conveyable, conveyance, conveyances, conveyor, conveyors

convince convinces, convinced, convincing, convincingly

cook cooks, cooked, cooking, cooker

cookie cookies

cool cools, cooled, cooling, cooler, coolest

cooperate cooperates, cooperated, cooperating, cooperative, cooperatively, cooperativeness, cooperation, cooperations

copper coppered, coppery

copy copies, copied, copying, copier, copiers

corn

corner corners, cornered, cornering

cornerstone cornerstones

corporation corporations, corporate, corporately

correct corrects, corrected, correcting, correction, corrections, correctly, correctness

correspond corresponds, corresponded, corresponding, correspondence, correspondent, correspondents

cost costs, costing, costly

costume costumes, costumed, costuming

cough coughs, coughed, coughing

could couldn't

council councils, councilor, councilors

counsel counsels, counseled, counseling, counselor, counselors

count counts, counted, counting, countless, countlessly, counter, counters

counteract counteracts, counteracted, counteracting, counteractive, counteraction, counteractions

country countries

county counties

coupon coupons

courage courageous, courageously

course courses, coursed

court courts, courted, courting

courtesy courtesies, courteous, courteously

cousin cousins

cover covers, covered, covering

cow cows

coward cowards, cowardly, cowardliness

crack cracks, cracked, cracking, cracker, crackers

crash crashes, crashed, crashing

crawl crawls, crawled, crawling, crawler, crawlers

crazy crazier, craziest, crazily, craziness

cream creams, creamed, creamy

create creates, created, creating, creation, creations, creative, creatively, creativeness, creativity, creator, creators

creature creatures

credence credential, credentials

credit credits, credited, crediting, creditor, creditors

creek creeks

creep creeps, crept, creeping, creeper, creepier, creepiest, creepily, creepiness, creepy

crime crimes, criminal, criminals, criminally

crimson crimsons, crimsoned

crisis crises

criticize criticizes, criticized, criticizing, critical, critically, critic, critics, criticism, criticisms, criticizer, critique, critiques

crop crops, cropped, cropping

cross crosses, crossed, crossing

crouch crouches, crouched, crouching

crowd crowds, crowded, crowding

cruel crueler, cruelest, cruelly, cruelty, cruelties, cruelness

crush crushes, crushed, crushing, crushable, crusher, crushers

cry cries, cried, crying, crier, criers

crystal crystals, crystallize

cultivate cultivates, cultivated, cultivating, cultivation, cultivator, cultivators

cunning cunningly, cunningness

cup cups

curious curiously, curiosity, curiosities, curiousness

current currents, currently

curtain curtains, curtained

curve curves, curved, curving

cushion cushions, cushioned, cushioning

custody custodies, custodial, custodian, custodians, custodianship, custodianships

custom customs, customary, customize, customizes, customized, customizing, customer, customers

cut cuts, cutting, cutter, cutters

cute cuter, cutest, cutely, cuteness

cyclone cyclones, cyclonic

cylinder cylinders, cylindric, cylindrical, cylindrically

D

dad dads, daddy

daily dailies

damage damages, damaged, damaging

dance dances, danced, dancing, dancer, dancers

danger dangers, dangerous, dangerously

dare dares, dared, daring, daringly

dark darker, darkest, darkish, darkly, darken, darkens, darkened, darkening, darkness

dash dashes, dashed, dashing

daughter daughters

dawn dawns, dawned, dawning

day days

deaf deafen, deafens, deafened, deafening, deafness

deal deals, dealt, dealing, dealings, dealer, dealers

dear dearer, dearest

death deaths, deathly

debate debates, debated, debating, debatable

debt debts, debtor, debtors

decade decades

deceive deceives, deceived, deceiving, deceit, deceitful, deceivable, deceptive, deceitfully, deceivingly, deceptively, deceitfulness, deception

December Dec.

decent decently, decency

decide decides, decided, deciding, decidedly, decisive, decisively, decision, decisions

decimal decimals

deck decks, decked, decking

declare declares, declared, declaring, declarative, declaration, declarations

decline declines, declined, declining, declinable

decorate decorates, decorated, decorating, decorator, decorators, decoration, decorations, decorative, decoratively, decorativeness

deed deeds, deeded

deep deeper, deepest, deeply, deepen

defeat defeats, defeated, defeating, defeatist

defect defects, defected, defecting, defective, defectively, defection, defections, defectiveness, defector, defectors

defend defends, defended, defending, defendable, defendant, defendants, defender, defenders

defense defenses, defensive, defensively, defensiveness, defenseless

define defines, defined, defining, definable, definite, definitely, definition, definitive, definitions

defy defies, defied, defying, defiant, defiantly, defiance

delay   delays, delayed, delaying

delicate   delicately, delicateness, delicacy, delicacies

delicious   deliciously, deliciousness

delight   delights, delighted, delightedly, delightful, delightfully, delightfulness

delirious   deliriously, delirium

deliver   delivers, delivered, delivering, deliverable, delivery, deliveries

demand   demands, demanded, demanding

democracy   democracies, democrat, democrats, democratic, democratically

demonstrate   demonstrates, demonstrated, demonstrating, demonstrator, demonstrators, demonstrative, demonstratively, demonstration, demonstrations

den   dens

dense   denser, densest, densely, denseness, density

dentist   dentists, dental, dentally, dentistry

deny   denies, denied, denying, denial, deniable

depart   departs, departed, departing, departure, departures

department   departments, departmental, departmentally

depend   depends, depended, depending, dependable, dependably, dependence, dependency, dependent, dependents

deposit   deposits, deposited, depositing, depositor, depositors

depot   depots

depth   depths

descend   descends, descended, descending, descendant, descendants, descender, decenders, descent

describe   describes, described, describing, describable, descriptive, descriptively, description, descriptions

desert   deserts, deserted, deserting, deserter, deserters, desertion, desertions

deserve   deserves, deserved, deserving, deservedly

design   designs, designed, designing, designer, designers

desire   desires, desired, desiring, desirable, desirably, desirous, desirously

desk   desks

desolate   desolated, desolately, desolateness, desolation

despair   despairs, despaired, despairing, despairingly

desperate   desperately, desperateness, desperation

despise   despises, despised, despising, despicable, despicably

dessert   desserts

destine   destines, destined, destining, destiny, destination, destinations

destroy destroys, destroyed, destroying, destroyer, destroyers

destruct destructs, destructed, destructing, destructive, destructible, destruction

determine determines, determined, determining, determinedly, determinable, determination, determinant, determinate

detour detours, detoured, detouring

develop develops, developed, developing, development, developments, developmental, developmentally, developer, developers

devour devours, devoured, devouring, devouringly

diameter diameters

diamond diamonds

dictionary dictionaries

die dies, died, dying

diet diets, dieted, dieting, dietary, dietetic, dieter, dieters, dietician, dieticians

differ differs, differed, differing, different, differently, difference, differences

difficult difficultly, difficulty, difficulties

dig digs, dug, digging, digger, diggers

digest digests, digested, digesting, digestible, digestion, digestive

dignity dignify, dignifies, dignified, dignifying, dignitary, dignitaries

dilapidate dilapidates, dilapidated, dilapidating, dilapidation

dilute   dilutes, diluted, diluting, dilution, dilutions

dim   dims, dimmed, dimming, dimly, dimmer, dimmest, dimness

dime   dimes

diminish   diminishes, diminished, diminishing, diminishable, diminutive

dine   dines, dined, dining, diner

dinner   dinners

dinosaur   dinosaurs

dip   dips, dipped, dipping, dipper, dippers

diploma   diplomas, diplomacy, diplomat, diplomats

direct   directs, directed, directing, directly, direction, directions, directional, directness, director, directors, directory, directorship

dirt   dirty, dirtier, dirtiest, dirties, dirtied, dirtying

disagree   disagreeable, disagreement, disagreements

disappear   disappears, disappeared, disappearing, disappearance

disappoint   disappoints, disappointed, disappointing, disappointment, disappointments

disaster   disasters, disastrous, disastrously

discipline   disciplines, disciplined, disciplining, disciplinary, disciplinarian, disciplinarians

disconnect disconnects, disconnected, disconnecting, disconnectedly, disconnection

discontinue discontinues, discontinued, discontinuing

discover discovers, discovered, discovering, discovery

discuss discusses, discussed, discussing, discussable, discussion, discussions

disease diseases, diseased

disgrace disgraces, disgraced, disgracing, disgraceful, disgracefully

disgust disgusts, disgusted, disgusting, disgustedly

dish dishes

dislike dislikes, disliked, disliking, dislikable

dislodge dislodges, dislodged, dislodging, dislodgment

dismal dismally

dismiss dismisses, dismissed, dismissing, dismissal

dispense dispenses, dispensed, dispensing, dispensable, dispensation, dispensary, dispenser, dispensers

dispose disposes, disposed, disposing, disposal, disposable, disposals, disposition, dispositions

displease displeases, displeased, displeasing, displeasingly, displeasure, displeasures

dispute disputes, disputed, disputing, disputable, disputably

disrupt disrupts, disrupted, disrupting, disruptive, disruptively, disruption, disruptions

dissatisfy dissatisfies, dissatisfied, dissatisfying, dissatisfactory, dissatisfaction

distant distantly, distance

distinct distinctly, distinctive, distinctively, distinction, distinctions, distinctiveness, distinctness

distinguish distinguishes, distinguished, distinguishing, distinguishable

distribute distributes, distributed, distributing, distributable, distribution, distributional, distributive, distributively

district districts

disturb disturbs, disturbed, disturbing, disturbingly, disturbance, disturbances

ditch ditches, ditched, ditching

dive dives, dived, diving, diver

divide divides, divided, dividing, divisible, divider, dividend, division, divisions, divisor

do did, does, done, doing, didn't, doesn't, don't, doer

doctor doctors, doctored, doctoring, Dr.

document documents, documented, documenting, documentation, documentations, documentary

dog dogs

doll dolls

dollar dollars

domestic domestics, domestically

donate donates, donated, donating, donation, donations, donor, donors

door doors

dose doses, dosage, dosages

dot dots, dotted, dotting

double doubles, doubled, doubling, doubly

doubt doubts, doubted, doubting, doubtingly, doubtable, doubtful, doubtfully, doubtfulness, doubtless, doubtlessly, doubtlessness, doubter, doubters

dove doves

down

downstairs

dozen dozens

drab drabber, drabbest, drably, drabness

draft drafts, drafted, drafting

drag drags, dragged, dragging

drain drains, drained, draining

drama dramatic, dramatical, dramatically, dramatics, dramatist, dramatists, dramatize, dramatizes, dramatizing, dramatization

drape drapes, draped, draping, drapery, draperies

draw   draws, drew, drawn, drawing, drawings

drawer   drawers

dream   dreams, dreamed, dreamt, dreaming, dreamer, dreamers, dreamy

dress   dresses, dressed, dressing, dressy

dresser   dressers

drill   drills, drilled, drilling

drink   drinks, drank, drunk, drinking, drinker, drinkers

drive   drives, drove, driving, driven, driver, drivers

drop   drops, dropped, dropping, dropper, droppers

drought   droughts

drown   drowns, drowned, drowning

drum   drums, drummed, drumming, drummer, drummers

dry   dries, dried, drying, drier, driest, dryly, dryness

dual   dually, dualistic, dualistically, dualism, duality

duck   ducks, ducked, ducking, duckling

due   dues

duplicate   duplicates, duplicated, duplicating, duplication, duplicator, duplicators

during

dust   dusts, dusted, dusting, dusty, duster, dusters

duty   duties, dutiful, dutifully

E

each

eager   eagerly, eagerness

ear   ears

early   earlier, earliest

earn   earns, earned, earning, earnings, earner, earners

earnest   earnestly, earnestness

earth   earthy, earthen, earthly

ease   eases, eased, easing

east   eastern, easterner, eastward, easterly

easy   easier, easiest, easily, easiness

easygoing   easygoingness

eat   eats, ate, eaten, eating

echo   echoes, echoed, echoing

economy   economies, economize, economizes, economized, economizing, economic, economics, economical, economically, economist, economists

edge   edges, edged, edging, edgy

edit   edits, edited, editing, editorial, editorials, editorially, edition, editions, editor, editors

educate   educates, educated, educating, educator, educators, education, educations, educational

effect   effects, effected, effecting, effective, effectively, effectiveness, effectual, effectually

efficient   efficiently, efficiency

effort   efforts, effortless, effortlessly

egg eggs

eight   eights, eighth

eighteen   eighteenth, eighteenths

eighty   eighties, eightieth

either

elaborate   elaborates, elaborated,
elaborating, elaborative, elaborately,
elaborateness, elaboration

elapse   elapses, elapsed, elapsing

elbow   elbows, elbowed, elbowing

elect   elects, elected, electing, elective,
electively, elector, electors, electoral,
electorate, election, elections, electioneer

electricity   electric, electrical, electrify,
electrifies, electrified, electrifying,
electrocute, electrocutes, electrocuted,
electrician, electricians

elegance   elegances, elegant, elegantly

element   elements

elephant   elephants

elevate   elevates, elevated, elevating,
elevation, elevations

elevator   elevators

eleven   elevens, eleventh

eligible   eligibly, eligibility

eliminate   eliminates, eliminated,
eliminating, elimination, eliminations

else

embarrass embarrasses, embarrassed, embarrassing, embarrassingly, embarrassment

emerge emerges, emerged, emerging, emergent, emergence, emergency, emergencies

emotion emotions, emotional, emotionally, emotionalism

emphasize emphasizes, emphasized, emphasizing, emphatic, emphatically, emphasis

empire empires, emperor, emperors, empress, empresses

employ employs, employed, employing, employable, employee, employees, employer, employers, employment

empty empties, emptied, emptying, emptiness

enable enables, enabled, enabling, enabler, enablers

enclose encloses, enclosed, enclosing, enclosure, enclosures

encounter encounters, encountered, encountering

encourage encourages, encouraged, encouraging, encouragingly, encouragement

end ends, ended, ending, endless

endorse endorses, endorsed, endorsing, endorser, endorsers, endorsement, endorsements

endure endures, endured, enduring, enduringly, endurable, endurably, endurance

enemy enemies

energy energies, energize, energizes, energized, energizing, energizer, energetic, energetically

enforce enforces, enforced, enforcing, enforceable, enforcer, enforcers, enforcement

engage engages, engaged, engaging, engagingly, engagement, engagements

engine engines, engineer, engineers, engineered, engineering

England English

enjoy enjoys, enjoyed, enjoying, enjoyable, enjoyably, enjoyment

enlarge enlarges, enlarged, enlarging, enlarger, enlargement, enlargements

enormous enormously, enormousness, enormity

enough

enter enters, entered, entering, entrance, entrances, entrant, entrants

entertain entertains, entertained, entertaining, entertainingly, entertainment, entertainer, entertainers

enthusiasm enthusiastic, enthusiastically, enthusiast, enthusiasts

entire entirely, entireness, entirety

envelope envelopes

envy   envies, envied, envying, envious,
   enviously, enviable, enviably

equal   equals, equaled, equaling, equality,
   equalize, equalizer, equalizers, equally

equip   equips, equipped, equipping,
   equipment

erect   erects, erected, erecting, erectly

erode   erodes, eroded, eroding, erosion

error   errors, errorless

escapade   escapades

escape   escapes, escaped, escaping, escapee,
   escapees

especially

essay   essays, essayist, essayists

essence   essences, essential, essentials,
   essentially

establish   establishes, established,
   establishing, establishment,
   establishments

estate   estates

estimate   estimates, estimated, estimating,
   estimation, estimations, estimator,
   estimators

even   evened, evenly, evenness, evener

evening   evenings

event   events, eventful, eventfully,
   eventual, eventually, eventuality

ever

every   everybody, everyone, everything, everywhere

evidence   evidences, evidenced, evidencing, evidential

evident   evidently

evil   evils, eviler, evilest, evilly, evilness

exact   exactly, exactness

examine   examines, examined, examining, exam, examination, examinations, examiner

example   examples

exceed   exceeds, exceeded, exceeding, exceedingly

excel   excels, excelled, excelling, excellence, excellency, excellent, excellently

except   excepts, excepted, excepting, exceptable, exception, exceptions, exceptionable, exceptionably, exceptional, exceptionally

excess   excesses, excessive, excessively, excessiveness

exchange   exchanges, exchanged, exchanging, exchangeable, exchanger, exchangers

excite   excites, excited, exciting, excitingly, excitable, excitably, excitedly, excitement

exclaim   exclaims, exclaimed, exclaiming, exclamation, exclamations, exclamatory

exclude   excludes, excluded, excluding, excludable, exclusive, exclusively, exclusion, exclusiveness

excursion excursions, excursioned, excursioning, excursionist

excuse excuses, excused, excusing, excusable

execute executes, executed, executing, executor, executors, execution, executions, executioner, executioners

executive executives

exercise exercises, exercised, exercising, exerciser

exhaust exhausts, exhausted, exhausting, exhaustible, exhaustive, exhaustively, exhaustion

exhibit exhibits, exhibited, exhibiting, exhibition, exhibitions, exhibitor, exhibitors

exile exiles, exiled, exiling

exist exists, existed, existing, existence, existences, existent

expect expects, expected, expecting, expectable, expectancy, expectant, expectantly, expectation, expectedly

expedite expedites, expedited, expediting, expeditionary, expeditious, expediter

expense expenses, expensive, expensively, expensiveness

experience experiences, experienced, experiencing, experiential, experientially

experiment experiments, experimented, experimenting, experimental, experimentation

expert experts, expertly, expertness

explain explains, explained, explaining, explainable, explanatory, explanatorily, explanation, explanations

explode explodes, exploded, exploding, explosion, explosive, explosives

explore explores, explored, exploring, explorer, explorers, exploration, exploratory

export exports, exported, exporting, exportation, exporter, exporters

expose exposes, exposed, exposing, exposure, exposures, exposition

express expresses, expressed, expressing, expression, expressions, expressionless, expressive, expressively, expressiveness

exquisite exquisitely, exquisiteness

extend extends, extended, extending, extensive, extensively, extension, extensions, extender, extenders

extent extents

external externally, externalize, externalizes, externalized, externalizing

extinct extinctive, extinction

extra extras

extraordinary extraordinarily

extravagance extravagances, extravagant, extravagantly, extravagancy, extravaganza

extreme extremes, extremely, extremeness, extremism, extremist, extremity

eye

eye   eyes, eyed, eyeing, eyeless

F

face faces, faced, facing, faceless

facile facilely, facilitate, facilitates, facilitated, facilitating, facilitation, facility, facilities

fact facts, factual, factually

factory factories

faculty faculties

fade fades, faded, fading

fail fails, failed, failing, failingly, failure, failures

faint faints, fainted, fainting, fainter, faintest, faintly

fair fairs, fairer, fairest, fairly, fairness

fall falls, fell, fallen, falling

false falsely, falsify, falsified, falsifying, falsehood

falter falters, faltered, faltering, falteringly

fame famed

familiar familiarly, familiarize, familiarizes, familiarized, familiarizing, familiarity, familiarities

family families

famous famously

fan fans, fanned, fanning

fancy fancies, fancied, fancying, fancier, fanciest, fanciful, fancifully

fantasy   fantasies, fantastic, fantastical, fantastically, fantasize, fantasizes, fantasized, fantasizing, fantasia

far   farther, farthest

fare   fares, fared, faring, farewell, farewells

farm   farms, farmed, farming, farmer, farmers

fascinate   fascinates, fascinated, fascinating, fascination, fascinations

fashion   fashions, fashioned, fashioning, fashionable, fashionably

fast   faster, fastest, fasten, fastens, fastened, fastening, fastener, fasteners

fat   fats, fatter, fattest, fattened, fattening, fatty

fatal   fatality, fatalities, fatally

fate   fates, fated, fateful

father   fathers

fault   faults, faulted, faulting, faultiness, faultless, faultlessly, faulty

fatigue   fatigues, fatigued, fatiguing, fatigable

favor   favors, favored, favoring, favorite, favorites, favorable, favorably, favorableness, favoritism

fear   fears, feared, fearing, fearful, fearfully, fearfulness, fearless, fearlessly, fearlessness

feast   feasts, feasted, feasting

feather   feathers, feathered, feathering, feathery

feature   features, featured, featuring

February   Feb.

federate   federates, federated, federating, federation, federations, federal, federally, federalist

feeble   feebler, feeblest, feebly, feebleness

feed   feeds, fed, feeding, feeder, feeders

feedback

feel   feels, felt, feeling, feelings

fence   fences, fenced, fencing, fencer, fencers

festive   festival, festivals, festively, festivity

fever   fevers, feverish

few   fewer, fewest

fiber   fibers, fibered, fibrous

field   fields

fiend   fiendish, fiendishly, fiendishness

fierce   fiercer, fiercest, fiercely, fierceness

fight   fights, fought, fighting, fighter, fighters

figure   figures, figured, figuring, figurine, figurines

file   files, filed, filing, filer, filers

fill   fills, filled, filling, filler, fillers

film   films, filmed, filming, filmy

final   finals, finalize, finalizes, finalized, finalizing, finally, finale, finales, finalist, finalists, finality

finance   finances, financed, financing, financial, financials, financially, financer, financers

find   finds, found, finding

fine   fines, fined, fining, finer, finest

finger   fingers, fingered, fingering

finish   finishes, finished, finishing

fir   firs

fire   fires, fired, firing, fiery

fireplace   fireplaces

firm   firms, firmed, firming, firmer, firmest, firmly, firmness

first   firstly

fish   fishes, fished, fishing, fishy, fishery

fit   fits, fitted, fitting, fitness

five   fives, fifth, fifths

fifteen   fifteenth, fifteenths

fifty   fifties, fiftieth

fix   fixes, fixed, fixing

flag   flags, flagged, flagging

flame   flames, flamed, flaming

flash   flashes, flashed, flashing, flashy, flasher, flashers

flashlight   flashlights

flat   flatten, flatter, flattest

flavor   flavors, flavored, flavoring, flavorful, flavorfully, flavorsome, flavorless, flavorlessly

fleck   flecks, flecked, flecking

flee   flees, fled, fleeing

flick   flicks, flicker, flickers, flickered, flickering

flight   flights

flinch   flinches, flinched, flinching

flock   flocks, flocked, flocking

flood   floods, flooded, flooding

floor   floors

flounder   flounders, floundered, floundering

flour   flours, floured, flouring, floury

flourish   flourishes, flourished, flourishing

flow   flows, flowed, flowing

flower   flowers, flowered, flowering

flu   influenza

flurry   flurries, flurried, flurrying

flutter   flutters, fluttered, fluttering, fluttery, flutterer

fly   flies, flew, flown, flying, flier, flyer, flyers

fold   folds, folded, folding, folder, folders

foliage   foliages, foliaged, foliate

follow   follows, followed, following, follower, followers

fond   fonder, fondest, fondly, fondness

food   foods

fool   fools, fooled, fooling, foolish, foolishly, foolishness

foot   feet

football   footballs

for   forever

forbid   forbids, forbidden, forbade, forbidding, forbiddance, forbiddingly

force   forces, forced, forcing, forceful, forcefully, forcible, forcibly, forcefulness

forehead   foreheads

foreign   foreigner, foreigners, foreignness

forest   forests, forested, forestry, forester, foresters

forfeit   forfeits, forfeited, forfeiting, forfeitable, forfeiter, forfeiters

forget   forgets, forgot, forgetting, forgetful, forgotten

fork   forks, forked, forking

form   forms, formed, forming, formerly, former

formal   formals, formally, formality, formalize, formation, formations

fort   forts, fortress

fortify   fortifies, fortified, fortifying, fortifier, fortification, fortifications

fortune   fortunes, fortunate, fortunately, fortuneless

forward   forwards, forwarded, forwarding, forwardness

foul   fouls, fouled, fouling, foulest

fountain   fountains

four   fours, fourth, fourths

fourteen   fourteens, fourteenth

forty   forties, fortieth

fox   foxes, foxy

fracture   fractures, fractured, fracturing

fragile   fragilely, fragility, fragilities

fragment   fragments, fragmented, fragmenting, fragmentary, fragmentation

fragrance   fragrant, fragrantly

frail   frailer, frailest, frailly, frailness, frailty

frame   frames, framed, framing, framer, framers

frank   franker, frankest, frankly, frankness

freckle   freckles, freckled, freckling

free   frees, freed, freeing, freer, freest, freely, freedom, freedoms

freeze   freezes, froze, freezing, frozen, freezer, freezers

freight   freighter, freighters

67

frequent frequents, frequented, frequenting, frequently, frequence, frequency, frequenter, frequentness

fresh fresher, freshest, freshly, freshness

Friday Fri.

friend friends, friendly, friendlier, friendliest, friendliness, friendless, friendship, friendships

fright frights, frighten, frightens, frightened, frightening, frighteningly, frightful, frightfully

frog frogs

from

front fronts, fronting

frontier frontiers

frost frosts, frosted, frosting, frosty

fry fries, fried, frying

fugitive fugitives, fugitively

full fuller, fullest, fully, fullness

fun funnier, funniest, funny, funnies

function functions, functioned, functioning, functional, functionally, functionary, functionaries

fundamental fundamentally, fundamentalist, fundamentalists

funeral funerals, funereal

fur furs, furry

furnace furnaces

furnish   furnishes, furnished, furnishing, furnishings, furnisher, furniture

further   furthers, furthered, furthering, furthest, furthermore

fury   furious, furiously, furor

future   futures, futuristic

G

gain gains, gained, gaining, gainful, gainfully

gallery galleries

gallon gallons

gallop gallops, galloped, galloping, galloper

game games, gaming

gang gangs, ganged, ganging

garage garages, garaged, garaging

garbage

garden gardens, gardened, gardening, gardener

gas gases

gasoline

gate gates

gather gathers, gathered, gathering, gatherings, gatherer

gear gears, geared, gearing

general generals, generalize, generalizes, generalized, generalizing, generalist, generality, generalities, generalization, generally

generate generates, generated, generating, generation, generations, generator

generosity generous, generously

genius geniuses

gentle gentler, gentlest, gently, gentleness

genuine   genuinely, genuineness

geography   geographies, geographic,
  geographical, geographer, geographers

germ   germs, germy

gesture   gestures, gestured, gesturing,
  gesturer

get   gets, got, getting, gotten

ghost   ghosts, ghostly

giant   giants, giantness

gift   gifts, gifted

gigantic   gigantically

gimmick   gimmicks, gimmicky, gimmickry

girl   girls

give   gives, gave, given, giving, giver

glad   gladder, gladdest, gladly, gladness

glance   glances, glanced, glancing

glare   glares, glared, glaring, glaringly

glass   glasses, glassy, glassful

glimmer   glimmers, glimmered,
  glimmering

glimpse   glimpses, glimpsed, glimpsing

glitter   glitters, glittered, glittering,
  glitteringly, glittery

globe   globes, global

gloom   gloomy, gloomier, gloomiest,
  gloomily, gloominess

glory   glories, gloried, glorying, glorify, glorifies, glorified, glorifying, glorifier, glorious, gloriously, gloriousness, glorification

glove   gloves

glow   glows, glowed, glowing

go   goes, went, going, gone

goat   goats

gold   golds, golden

golf   golfs, golfing, golfer

good   goodness

good-bye   good-byes

goose   geese

gopher   gophers

gorgeous   gorgeously, gorgeousness

gossip   gossips, gossiped, gossiping, gossipy, gossiper

govern   governs, governed, governing, governor, governors, government, governments, governess, governable

gown   gowns

grab   grabs, grabbed, grabbing

grace   graces, graced, gracing, graceful, gracefully, gracefulness, gracious, graciousness, graceless, gracelessly

grade   grades, graded, grading, grader

gradual   gradually, gradualness

graduate   graduates, graduated, graduating, graduation, graduations

grain   grains, grainy

grammar   grammarian, grammatical,
   grammatically

grand   grander, grandest, grandness,
   grandly

grandfather   grandfathers

grandmother   grandmothers

grape   grapes

grapefruit   grapefruits

grasp   grasps, grasped, grasping

grass   grasses, grassy

grateful   gratefully, gratefulness

gratify   gratifies, gratified, gratifying,
   gratifier, gratitude

gravel   gravels, graveled, graveling,
   gravelly

gray   grayer, grayest

graze   grazes, grazed, grazing

grease   greases, greased, greasing, greasy,
   greasier, greasiest, greasiness

great   greater, greatest, greatly, greatness

green   greener, greenest

greet   greets, greeted, greeting, greeter

grief   grieve, grieves, grieved, grieving,
   grievingly, grievous, grievously,
   grievance, griever

grim   grimmer, grimmest, grimly

grind   grinds, grinding, grinder

grip

grip   grips, gripped, gripping

groan   groans, groaned, groaning

grocery   groceries, grocer

groove   grooves, grooved, grooving, groovy

gross   grosses, grossly, grossness

ground   grounds, grounded

group   groups, grouped, grouping

grow   grows, grew, growing, grown, growth, growths, grower, growers

growl   growls, growled, growling, growler

gruff   gruffly, gruffness

guarantee   guarantees, guaranteed, guaranteeing, guaranty

guard   guards, guarded, guarding, guardedly, guardingly

guardian   guardians, guardianship

guess   guesses, guessed, guessing, guesser

guide   guides, guided, guiding, guider, guidance

gulf   gulfs

gush   gushes, gushed, gushing

gymnasium   gymnasiums, gymnast, gymnastic, gymnastics, gym

H

habit   habits

hair   hairs, hairy, hairless

half   halves

hall   halls

Halloween

hammer   hammers, hammered, hammering

hand   hands, handful, handfuls

handkerchief   handkerchiefs

handle   handles, handled, handling, handler

handsome   handsomer, handsomest,
handsomely, handsomeness

handy   handier, handiest, handily, handiness

hang   hangs, hanged, hung, hanging, hanger

happen   happens, happened, happening

happy   happier, happiest, happily,
happiness

harbor   harbors, harbored, harboring

hard   harder, hardest, hardly

hardware   hardwares

harm   harms, harmed, harming, harmful,
harmless, harmlessness

harmony   harmonize, harmonizes,
harmonized, harmonizing, harmonies,
harmonious, harmoniously,
harmoniousness, harmonics, harmonist

harry   harries, harried, harrying

harvest   harvests, harvested, harvesting, harvester

haste   hastens, hasten, hastened, hastening, hasty, hastily

hat   hats

hatch   hatches, hatched, hatching, hatchery

hate   hates, hated, hating, hateful, hatefully

haunt   haunts, haunted, haunting, hauntingly

have   has, had, having, hasn't, hadn't

he   he's, him, his

head   heads, headed, heading

headache   headaches

headquarters

heal   healer, healers

health   healthy, healthier, healthiest, healthful, healthfully, healthily, healthiness, healthfulness

heap   heaps, heaped, heaping

hear   hears, heard, hearing

heart   hearts

hearty   heartier, heartiest

heat   heats, heated, heating, heater

heavy   heavier, heaviest, heavily, heaviness

hedge   hedges, hedged, hedging

heel   heels, heeled, heeling

height   heights, heighten, heightens, heightened, heightening

helicopter   helicopters

hello   hellos

helmet   helmets, helmeted

help   helps, helped, helping, helpful, helpfully, helpfulness, helpless, helper

hen   hens

her

herd   herds, herded, herder, herding

here

hermit   hermits, hermetic, hermitage

hero   heroes, heroic, heroism

herself

hesitate   hesitates, hesitated, hesitating, hesitatingly, hesitant, hesitater, hesitation

hide   hides, hid, hiding, hidden

high   higher, highest, highly, highness

highway   highways

hike   hikes, hiked, hiking, hiker

hill   hills, hilly

him

himself

hinder   hinders, hindered, hindering, hindrance

hindsight

hinge   hinges, hinged, hinging

hire   hires, hired, hiring

history   histories, historic, historical, historically, historian

hit   hits, hitting, hitter

hitch   hitches, hitched, hitching

hobby   hobbies, hobbyist

hold   holds, held, holding, holdings, holder, holders

hole   holes, holey

holiday   holidays

home   homes

homesick   homesickness

honest   honestly, honesty

honey   honeys, honeyed

honor   honors, honored, honoring, honorable, honorably, honorarily, honorary

hook   hooks, hooked, hooking

hop   hops, hopped, hopping

hope   hopes, hoped, hoping, hopeful, hopefully, hopefulness, hopeless, hopelessly, hopelessness

horizon   horizons

horizontal   horizontally

horn   horns

horror   horrors, horrible, horribly, horribleness, horrify, horrifies, horrified, horrifying, horrifyingly, horrid, horridly, horridness

horse   horses

horseback

hose   hoses, hosed, hosing

hostile   hostilely, hostility, hostilities

hot   hotter, hottest

hotel   hotels

hour   hours, hourly, hr.

house   houses

household   households, householder

how

however

howl   howls, howled, howling, howler

hug   hugs, hugged, hugging

huge   huger, hugest, hugely, hugeness

human   humans, humanly, humane,
   humanely, humanitarian, humanity,
   humanness, humanist, humanism

humiliate   humiliates, humiliated,
   humiliating, humiliation, humility

humor   humors, humored, humoring,
   humorous, humorously, humorist,
   humorists

hundred   hundreds, hundredth

hunger   hungers, hungered, hungering,
   hungry, hungrier, hungriest, hungrily,
   hungriness

hunt   hunts, hunted, hunting, hunter,
   hunters

hurdle   hurdles, hurdled, hurdling, hurdler

hurry

hurry   hurries, hurried, hurrying

hurt   hurts, hurting, hurtful

husband husbands

hygiene   hygienic, hygienically, hygienist

I

I I'd, I'll, I'm, I've

ice ices, iced, icing, icy, icicle, icicles

ice cream ice creams

idea ideas

ideal ideals, ideally, idealism, idealist, idealistic

identical identically, identicalness

idle idles, idled, idling, idly, idleness, idler

i f

ignore ignores, ignored, ignoring, ignorant, ignorantly, ignorance

ill illness

illusion illusions, illusionary, illusionist

illustrate illustrates, illustrated, illustrating, illustration, illustrative, illustrious, illustriously, illustrator

image images, imagine, imagines, imagined, imagining, imagination, imaginations, imaginative, imaginary, imagery

imitate imitates, imitated, imitating, imitation, imitative, imitator

immediate immediately, immediacy

immense immensely, immensity, immenseness

impersonate impersonates, impersonated, impersonating, impersonation, impersonator

imply

imply   implies, implied, implying, implicit, implication

import   imports, imported, importing, importable, importer, importation

important   importantly, importance

impose   imposes, imposed, imposing, imposingly, imposer, imposition

impossible   impossibly, impossibility, impossibilities

impress   impresses, impressed, impressing, impression, impressions, impressionable, impressive, impressively, impressionism, impressionist

improbable   improbably, improbability

improve   improves, improved, improving, improvable, improvement, improvements

improvise   improvises, improvised, improvising, improviser, improvisation

impulse   impulses, impulsive, impulsively

in

inch   in., inched, inches, inching

incident   incidents, incidental, incidentally, incidence

incite   incites, incited, inciting, incitement

incline   inclines, inclined, inclining, inclination

include   includes, included, including, inclusive, inclusion

income   incomes, incoming

inconvenience inconveniences, inconvenienced, inconveniencing, inconvenient, inconveniently, inconveniency

increase increases, increased, increasing, increasingly

indeed

indefinite indefinitely, indefiniteness

independent independence, independently, independency

Indian Indians

indicate indicates, indicated, indicating, indicator, indication

indict indicts, indicted, indicting, indictable, indictment

indifferent indifferently, indifference

indirect indirectly, indirection, indirectness

individual individuals, individually, individualist, individuality, individualize

indoor indoors

industry industries, industrial, industrious, industriously, industrialize, industrialism, industrialist

ineligible ineligibly, ineligibility

inevitable inevitably, inevitability

infant infants, infantile, infancy

inferior inferiority

inflame inflames, inflamed, inflaming, inflammable, inflammatory, inflammation

inflate   inflates, inflated, inflating, inflatable, inflation, inflationary, inflationist

inflict   inflicts, inflicted, inflicting, inflicter, infliction

influence   influences, influenced, influencing, influential

inform   informs, informed, informing, informative, information, informational, informer

infrequent   infrequently, infrequence, infrequency, infrequentness

inhabit   inhabits, inhabited, inhabiting, inhabitant, inhabitants

initial   initials, initialed, initialing, initially

initiate   initiates, initiated, initiating, initiative, initiation, initiator

inject   injects, injected, injecting, injectable, injection, injector

injure   injures, injured, injuring, injurious, injuriously, injury, injuries

ink   inks, inked, inky

inning   innings

innocent   innocence, innocently

input

inquire   inquires, inquired, inquiring, inquiringly, inquiry, inquiries, inquisition, inquisitions

insect   insects, insecticide

inside   insides, insider, insiders

insist   insists, insisted, insisting, insistent, insistently

inspect   inspects, inspected, inspecting, inspection, inspections, inspector

inspire   inspires, inspired, inspiring, inspiration, inspirational

install   installs, installed, installing, installment, installation

instant   instantaneous, instantaneously, instantly, instance

instead

instinct   instincts, instinctual, instinctive, instinctively

institute   institutes, instituted, instituting, institution, institutions, institutional, institutionalize

instruct   instructs, instructed, instructing, instruction, instructions, instructional, instructive, instructively, instructor, instructors

instrument   instruments, instrumental, instrumentally, instrumentalist

insulate   insulates, insulated, insulating, insulation

insult   insults, insulted, insulting

insure   insures, insured, insuring, insurable, insurer, insurers, insurance

integrate   integrates, integrated, integrating, integrative, integration

intellect intellects, intellectual, intellectually intellectualist, intellectualize

intelligence intelligent, intelligently, intelligible, intelligibly, intelligibility

intend intends, intended, intending, intent, intention, intentions, intentional, intentionally, intently, intents

intense intensely, intenseness, intensify, intensive, intensiveness, intensively

intercept intercepts, intercepted, intercepting, interception, interceptor, interceptors

interest interests, interested, interesting, interestingly

interfere interferes, interfered, interfering, interference

interior interiors

internal internally, internalize, internalizes, internalized, internalizing, internalization

international internationally

interpret interprets, interpreted, interpreting

interrupt interrupts, interrupted, interrupting, interruption, interruptive, interrupter

interval intervals

interview interviews, interviewed, interviewing, interviewer, interviewee

intimate intimately, intimacy

into

introduce introduces, introduced,
introducing, introductory, introduction,
introductions

intrude intrudes, intruded, intruding,
intrusive, intrusion, intruder

invade invades, invaded, invading, invasive,
invasion, invasions, invader

invent invents, invented, inventing,
inventive, inventively, inventiveness,
invention, inventions, inventor

invest invests, invested, investing,
investor, investment

investigate investigates, investigated,
investigating, investigator, investigators,
investigation

invisible invisibly, invisibleness

invite invites, invited, inviting, invitation,
invitations

involuntary involuntarily

involve involves, involved, involving,
involvement

iron irons, ironed, ironing

irony ironies, ironic, ironical, ironically

irrigate irrigates, irrigated, irrigating,
irrigation

irritate irritates, irritated, irritating,
irritative, irritable, irritably, irritant,
irritation

island islands, islander

isolate

isolate   isolates, isolated, isolating,
    isolation, isolationist, isolationists

issue   issues, issued, issuing, issuable

it   it's

item   items, itemize, itemizes, itemized,
    itemizing, itemization

itself

J

jacket   jackets

jail   jails, jailed, jailing, jailer, jailers

January   Jan.

jar   jars, jarred, jarring

jealous   jealously, jealousy, jealousies, jealousness

jell   jells, jelled, jelling, jelly, jellies, jellied, jellying

jest   jests, jested, jesting, jester, jesters

jet   jets, jetted, jetting

jewel   jewels, jeweled, jeweling, jewelry, jeweler, jewelers

jilt   jilts, jilted, jilting

job   jobs

join   joins, joined, joining, joiner, joiners

joint   joints, jointed, jointly

joke   jokes, joked, joking, jokingly, joker, jokers

jolly   jollier, jolliest

journal   journals, journalism, journalist, journalists

journey   journeys, journeyed, journeying

joy   joyful, joyous, joyless, joyously

jubilant   jubilantly, jubilate, jubilates, jubilated, jubilating, jubilation, jubilance

judge   judges, judged, judging, judgment, judgments, judgmental

juice   juices, juiced, juicing, juicy, juicier, juiciest, juiciness

July

jump   jumps, jumped, jumping, jumpy, jumpier, jumpiest

June

jungle   jungles

junior   juniors, Jr.

jury   juries, juror, jurors

just   justly, justness, justice, justify, justified, justifying, justification

K

keep   keeps, kept, keeping, keeper, keepers

kettle   kettles

kick   kicks, kicked, kicking, kicker, kickers

kid   kids, kidded, kidding, kidder, kidders

kind   kinder, kindest, kindly, kindness

kindle   kindles, kindled, kindling

king   kings, kingly, kingdom, kingdoms

kitchen   kitchens

kite   kites

kitten   kittens, kitty, kitties

knee   knees, kneel, kneels, knelt, kneeled, kneeling

knife   knifes, knifed, knifing, knives

knight   knights, knighted, knighting, knightly

knit   knits, knitted, knitting, knitter, knitters

knock   knocks, knocked, knocking, knocker

knot   knots, knotted, knotting, knotty

know   knows, knew, known, knowing, knowingly, knowledge, knowledgeable, knowledgeably

L

labor labors, labored, laboring, laborious, laboriously, laborer, laborers

laboratory laboratories, lab, labs

lace laces, laced, lacing, lacy

ladder ladders

lady ladies

lake lakes

lamb lambs

lamp lamps

land lands, landed, landing, landings

landlord landlords

landscape landscapes, landscaped, landscaping, landscaper, landscapers

landslide landslides

language languages

lantern lanterns

large larger, largest, largely, largeness

last lasts, lasted, lasting, lastingly, lastly, lastingness

late later, latest, lately, lateness

latter latterly

laugh laughs, laughed, laughing, laughable, laughter

launch launches, launched, launching, launcher, launchers

laundry   laundries, launder, launders, laundered, laundering, launderer, laundromat

law   laws, lawful, lawless, lawyer, lawyers

lawn   lawns

lay   lays, laid, lain, laying

lazy   lazier, laziest, lazily, laziness

lead   leads, led, leading, leader, leaders

leaf   leaves, leafy

league   leagues

leak   leaks, leaked, leaking, leaky

lean   leans, leaned, leaning, leaner, leanest

learn   learns, learned, learning, learner, learners

lease   leases, leased, leasing

leash   leashes, leashed, leashing

leather   leathers, leathered, leathery

leave   leaves, left, leaving

leeway   leeways

leg   legs

legal   legally, legality, legalize, legalizes, legalized, legalizing, legalization

legion   legions, legionary, legionnaire, legionnaires

legislate   legislates, legislated, legislating, legislator, legislators, legislature, legislatures, legislation, legislative

leisure   leisurely, leisureliness

lemon   lemons, lemony

lemonade

lend   lends, lent, lending, lender, lenders

length   lengths, lengthen, lengthens, lengthened, lengthening, lengthy, lengthier, lengthiest

less   lesser, least, lessen, lessens, lessened, lessening

lesson   lessons

let   lets, letting

letter   letters, lettered, lettering

lettuce

levee   levees, leveed, leveeing

level   levels, leveled, leveling, levelness, leveler, levelers

levy   levies, levied, levying

liable   liability, liabilities

libel   libels, libeled, libeling, libelous

liberate   liberates, liberated, liberating, liberation, liberty, liberties, liberal, liberator, liberators

library   libraries, librarian, librarians

license   licenses, licensed, licensing

lie   lies, lied, lying, liar, liars, lay, lain

lieutenant   lieutenants

life   lifeless, lifelessness

lift   lifts, lifted, lifting, lifter, lifters

light   lights, lighted, lit, lighting, lightly, lighter, lightest, lightness, lighten, lightened

lightning

like   likes, liked, liking, likely, likelier, likeliest, likeliness, likable, liken, likeness

limb   limbs

limber   limbers, limbered, limbering

limit   limits, limited, limiting, limitless, limitation, limitations

limp   limps, limped, limping

line   lines, lined, lining, liner, liners

linen   linens

linger   lingers, lingered, lingering, lingerer, lingerers

lion   lions, lioness

liquid   liquids, liquefy, liquefies, liquefied, liquefying, liquidity, liquidness

list   lists, listed, listing

listen   listens, listened, listening, listener, listeners

literature   literatures, literate, literately, literacy, literary, literateness

little   littler, littlest

live   lives, lived, living, lively, livelier, liveliest, livable

load   loads, loaded, loading, loader, loaders

loaf   loafs, loafed, loafing, loafer, loafers

loan

loan loans, loaned, loaning

local locally, localize, localizes, localized, localizing, locale, locales, locality, localities, localization

locate locates, located, locating, location, locations

lock locks, locked, locking

lodge lodges, lodged, lodging, lodger, lodgers

log logs, logging, logger, loggers

logic logical, logically, logicalness, logician

loiter loiters, loitered, loitering, loiterer, loiterers

lone lonely, lonelier, loneliest, lonesome, loner, loners, loneliness

long longer, longest

look looks, looked, looking, looker, lookers

loop loops, looped, looping

loose loosen, loosens, loosened, loosening, looser, loosest, loosely, looseness

lose loses, lost, losing, loser, losers, loss, losses

lot lots

loud louder, loudest, loudly, loudness

love loves, loved, loving, lovable, lovely, lovelier, loveliest, loveliness

low lower, lowest

loyal loyally, loyalty, loyalties, loyalism, loyalist

luck lucky, luckier, luckiest, luckily

lump   lumps, lumped, lumping, lumpy, lumpier, lumpiest, lumpiness

lunch   lunches, lunched, lunching, luncheon, luncheons

lung   lungs

lunge   lunges, lunged, lunging, lunger, lungers

luscious   lusciously, lusciousness

luster   lusters, lustered, lustering, lustrous, lustrously

luxury   luxuries, luxurious, luxuriously, luxuriant

lyric   lyrics, lyrical, lyricism, lyricist, lyricists

M

machine machines, machinery, machinist, machinists

mad madder, maddest, madden, maddens, maddened, maddening, madly, madness

magazine magazines

magic magical, magically, magician, magicians

magnificence magnificent, magnificently

mail mails, mailed, mailing, mailer, mailers

maintain maintains, maintained, maintaining, maintainable, maintenance

majesty majesties, majestic, majestical, majestically

major majors, majored, majoring, majority, majorities

make makes, made, making

malfunction malfunctions, malfunctioned, malfunctioning

mammal mammals

man men

manage manages, managed, managing, manageable, manager, managers, management

maneuver maneuvers, maneuvered, maneuvering, maneuverable, maneuverability

98

manipulate   manipulates, manipulated, manipulating, manipulative, manipulatory, manipulation, manipulator, manipulators

manner   manners, mannered, mannerly, mannerism, mannerisms

mansion   mansions

manual   manuals, manually

manufacture   manufactures, manufactured, manufacturing, manufacturer, manufacturers

many

map   maps, mapped, mapping

marathon   marathon, marathoner, marathoners

marble   marbles, marbled, marbling

March   Mar.

margin   margins, margined, margining, marginal, marginally

mark   marks, marked, marking, marker, markers

marry   marries, married, marrying, marriage, marriages

marvel   marvels, marveled, marveling, marvelous, marvelously

mascot   mascots

mask   masks, masked, masking

mass   masses, massed, massing, massive, massively, massiveness

massage massages, massaged, massaging, massager, massagers

master masters, mastered, mastering, masterful, masterfully, masterly, mastery

mat mats, matted, matting

match matches, matched, matching, matchless

material materials, materialize, materializes, materialized, materializing

maternal maternally, maternity

mathematics mathematical, mathematically, mathematician, mathematicians, math

matter matters, mattered

mature matures, matured, maturing, maturely, maturate, maturation

May

maybe may

mayor mayors, mayoral

me

meadow meadows

meal meals

mean means, meant, meaning, meaningful, meaningless, meaner, meanest, meanly, meanness

meantime

meanwhile

measure measures, measured, measuring, measurable, measurably, measurement, measurements

meat meats, meaty, meatier, meatiest

mechanize mechanizes, mechanized, mechanizing, mechanization mechanism, mechanisms, mechanic, mechanics, mechanical, mechanically

medal medals, medalist, medallion, medallions

medicine medicines, medicinal, medical, medically, medicate, medicates, medicated, medicating, medication, medications, medic, medics

medium mediums, media, median

meet meets, met, meeting

melt melts, melted, melting

member members, membership, memberships

membrane membranes, membraned, membranous

memory memories, memorize, memorizes, memorized, memorizing, memorization, memorable, memorably, memorial, memorials, memorialize, memorabilia, memoir, memoirs

memorandum memoranda, memo, memos

mention mentions, mentioned, mentioning, mentionable

merchant merchants, merchandise, merchandises, merchandised, merchandising, merchandiser

mere   merest, merely

merit   merits, merited, meriting, meritorious

merry   merrier, merriest, merrily, merriness

message   messages, messenger, messengers

metal   metals, metallic

meter   meters, metered, metering, metric, metrics, metrical, metrically

method   methods

metropolis   metropolitan

middle   mid, midst

midnight   midnights

might   mighty, mightier, mightiest, mightily, mightiness

migrate   migrates, migrated, migrating, migratory, migration, migrant, migrants, migrator, migrators

mild   milder, mildest, mildly, mildness

mile   miles, mileage

milk   milks, milked, milking, milky

mill   mills, miller, millers

million   millions, millionth, millionaire, millionaires

mimic   mimics, mimicked, mimicking, mimicry

mind   minds, minded, minding

mine   mines, mined, mining, miner, miners

mineral   minerals, mineralize, mineralizes, mineralized, mineralizing, mineralogy, mineralogist, mineralogists

minimum   minimums, minimal, minimize

minor   minors, minored, minoring, minority, minorities

mint   mints, minted, minting, minty

minute   minutes, min., mins.

mirror   mirrors, mirrored, mirroring

miscalculate   miscalculates, miscalculated, miscalculating, miscalculation, miscalculations

mischief   mischievous, mischievously

misery   miseries, miserable, miserably, miserableness

misinterpret   misinterprets, misinterpreted, misinterpreting, misinterpretation, misinterpretations

miss   misses, missed, missing

misspell   misspells, misspelled, misspelling, misspeller, misspellers

mist   mists, misted, misting, misty

mistake   mistakes, mistook, mistaking, mistaken, mistakenly, mistakable

misuse   misuses, misused, misusing, misusage

mix   mixes, mixed, mixing, mixer, mixers, mixture, mixtures

model   models, modeled, modeling

modest   modestly, modesty

modify   modifies, modified, modifying, modifiable, modification, modifications, modifier, modifiers

moist   moisten, moistens, moistened, moistening, moisture, moistness, moisturize, moisturizes, moisturized, moisturizing

molten

mom   moms, mommy

moment   moments, momentary, momentous, momentarily

Monday   Mon.

money   moneys, monies

monkey   monkeys

monopoly   monopolies, monopolize, monopolizes, monopolized, monopolizing, monopolist, monopolists, monopolistic, monopolizer, monopolizers

monster   monsters, monstrous, monstrously, monstrosity, monstrosities

month   months, monthly, bimonthly

monument   monuments, monumental, monumentally

mood   moods, moody, moodier, moodiest, moodily, moodiness

moon   moons

moral   morals, moralistic, moralistically, morally, moralize, moralizes, moralized, moralizing, moralism, morale, morality, moralist, moralists

more   most, mostly

morning mornings

mortal mortally, mortality

mortgage mortgages, mortgaged, mortgaging, mortgagee, mortgagees, mortgager, mortgagers

mosquito mosquitoes

moss mosses, mossy

mother mothers

motion motions, motioned, motioning, motionless

motive motives, motivate, motivates, motivated, motivating, motivation, motivator, motivators

motor motors, motored, motoring, motorize, motorist, motorists

motto mottos

mount mounts, mounted, mounting

mountain mountains, mountainous, mountaineer, mountaineers, mountainside

mourn mourns, mourned, mourning, mournful, mournfully, mourner, mourners

mouse mice, mousy

mouth mouths, mouthful

move moves, moved, moving, movable, mover, movers, movement

movie movies

much

mud

mud   muddy, muddies, muddied, muddying, muddier, muddiest, muddiness

multiply   multiplies, multiplied, multiplying, multiple, multiples, multiplication, multiplier, multipliers

multitude   multitudes, multitudinous

mural   murals

murmur   murmurs, murmured, murmuring

muscle   muscles, muscled, muscling, muscular

museum   museums

music   musical, musicals, musically, musician, musicians

must

mustard   mustards

mutilate   mutilates, mutilated, mutilating, mutilation, mutilator, mutilators

my

myself

mystery   mysteries, mysterious, mysteriously

mystify   mystifies, mystified, mystifying, mystification

N

nail   nails, nailed, nailing

name   names, named, naming, namely

nap   naps, napped, napping

narrate   narrates, narrated, narrating, narrative, narratives, narration, narrations, narrator, narrators

nation   nations, national, nationally, nationalist, nationality, nationalities

natural   naturally, naturalistic, naturalness, naturalize, naturalized, naturalizing, naturalist, naturalists

nature   natures, natured

naughty   naughtier, naughtiest, naughtily, naughtiness

navy   navies, naval

near   nears, neared, nearing, nearer, nearest, nearness, nearly

nearby

neat   neater, neatest, neatly, neatness

necessary   necessarily, necessitate, necessitates, necessitated, necessitating, necessity, necessities

neck   necks

necktie   neckties

need   needs, needed, needing, needy, needier, neediest, needless, needlessly, needlessness

needle

needle needles, needled, needling, needler,
  needlers

neglect neglects, neglected, neglecting,
  neglectful, neglectfully, negligent,
  negligence, negligible

neighbor neighbors, neighboring,
  neighborliness, neighborly, neighborhood,
  neighborhoods

neither

nephew nephews

nerve nerves, nerved, nerving, nervous,
  nervously, nervousness, nervy, nervier,
  nerviest

nest nests, nesting, nester, nesters

net nets, netting

never

new newer, newest, newly

newsletter newsletters

newspaper newspapers

next

nice nicer, nicest, nicely

nickel nickels

niece nieces

night nights, nightly

nine nines, ninth, ninths

nineteen nineteens, nineteenth

no none, not, nothing

noble nobler, noblest, nobly, nobles, nobility, nobleness

nobody

noise noises, noisy, noisier, noisiest, noisily, noisiness

nonsense nonsensical, nonsensically

noodle noodles

noon noons

normal normally, normalize, normalized, normalizing, normalcy, normality

north northerly, northern, northerner, northward

nose noses, nosy

note notes, noted, noting, notable, notably, notate, notates, notated, notating, notation, notations

notebook notebooks

notice notices, noticed, noticing, noticeable, noticeably, notify, notifies, notified, notifying

notorious notoriously, notoriety

novel novels, novelize, novelist, novelists

novelty novelties

November Nov.

now

nowhere

nuisance nuisances

numb numbs, numbed, numbing, numbly

number

number   numbers, numbered, numbering

numeral   numerals, numerate, numerates,
   numerated, numerating, numeration,
   numerator, numerators, numeric,
   numerical, numerically, numerous

nurse   nurses, nursed, nursing, nursery

nut   nuts, nutty

O

o'clock

oak oaks

obey obeys, obeyed, obeying, obedient, obedience, obediently

object objects, objected, objecting, objection, objectionable, objectionably

obligate obligates, obligated, obligating, obligatory, obligation, obligations

oblige obliges, obliged, obliging

observe observes, observed, observing, observation, observations, observational, observable, observatory, observatories, observant, observer, observers

obtain obtains, obtained, obtaining, obtainable, obtainment

obvious obviously, obviousness

occasion occasions, occasioned, occasioning, occasional, occasionally

occupy occupies, occupied, occupying, occupant, occupants, occupation, occupations, occupational

occur occurs, occurred, occurring, occurrence, occurrences

ocean oceans

October Oct.

odd odds, odder, oddest, oddly, oddity, oddness

odor odors, odorous

of

off

offend offends, offended, offending, offender, offenders

offense offenses, offensive, offensively, offensiveness

offer offers, offered, offering

office offices, official, officials, officially, officiate, officer, officers, officiary

often oftener, oftenest

oh

oil oils, oiled, oiling, oily, oiler, oilers

old older, oldest, oldster, oldsters

omit omits, omitted, omitting, omisive, omissible, omission, omissions

on

once

one

onion onions

only

open opens, opened, opening, openings, opener, openers, openly

opera operas, operetta, operettas, operatic

operate operates, operated, operating, operation, operations, operational, operator, operators

opinion opinions, opinionated

opportunity   opportunities, opportunist, opportunists, opportunistic, opportune, opportunely, opportunism

oppose   opposes, opposed, opposing, opposite, opposites, oppositely, opposition, oppositeness

optimism   optimistic, optimistically, optimist, optimists

option   options, optioned, optional, optionally

or

orange   oranges

orbit   orbits, orbited, orbiting, orbital, orbiter, orbiters

orchard   orchards

orchestra   orchestras, orchestrate, orchestrates, orchestrated, orchestrating, orchestration, orchestrations

order   orders, ordered, ordering, orderly, orderlies

ordinary   ordinarily, ordinariness

ore   ores

organ   organs, organist, organists

organic   organism, organisms, organically

organize   organizes, organized, organizing, organizer, organizers, organization, organizations

origin   origins, original, originals, originally, originate, originates, originality, originator, originators

ornament   ornaments, ornamented, ornamenting, ornamental, ornamentally, ornamentation, ornamentations

other   others, otherwise

ought

ounce   ounces, oz.

our   ours, ourselves

out   outs

outdoor   outdoors

outfit   outfits, outfitted, outfitting, outfitter, outfitters

outline   outlines, outlined, outlining

outside   outsides, outsider, outsiders

oval   ovals

over

overcome   overcomes, overcame, overcoming

overflow   overflows, overflowed, overflowing, overflowingly

oversight   oversights

overture   overtures

overturn   overturns, overturned, overturning

owe   owes, owed, owing

owl   owls, owlish, owlet, owlets

own   owns, owned, owning, owner, owners, ownership

oyster   oysters

P

pack packs, packed, packing, packer, packers

package packages, packaged, packaging

paddle paddles, paddled, paddling

page pages, paged, paging, paginate, pagination

pageant pageants, pageantry, pageantries

pail pails

pain pains, pained, painful, painfully, painfulness, painless, painlessly, painlessness

paint paints, painted, painting, painter, painters

pair pairs, paired, pairing

pajamas

palace palaces

palm palms, palmed, palming, palmist, palmists, palmistry

pamphlet pamphlets, pamphleteer, pamphleteers

pan pans, panned, panning

pants

paper papers, papered, papering

parade parades, paraded, parading

paradise paradises

paragraph paragraphs, paragraphed, paragraphing

parallel   parallels, paralleled, parralleling

parcel   parcels, parceled, parceling

pardon   pardons, pardoned, pardoning, pardonable

parent   parents, parental

park   parks, parked, parking

part   parts, parted, parting, partly, partial, partially

participate   participates, participated, participating, participation, participant, participants

particular   particulars, particularly, particularity

partner   partners, partnership

party   parties, partied, partying, partyer, partyers

pass   passes, passed, passing, passer, passers

passage   passages, passaged, passaging, passenger, passengers

past   pasts

paste   pastes, pasted, pasting, pasty

pasture   pastures, pastured, pasturing

pat   pats, patted, patting

patch   patches, patched, patching

patent   patents, patented, patenting

path   paths

pathway   pathways

patience   patient, patients, patiently

pattern   patterns, patterned, patterning

pause   pauses, paused, pausing

pave   paves, paved, paving, pavement, pavements

pay   pays, paid, paying, payable, payment, payments

peace   peaceful, peacefully, peacefulness

peanut   peanuts

peculiar   peculiarly, peculiarity, peculiarities

peek   peeks, peeked, peeking

peer   peers, peered, peering

pen   pens, penned, penning

pencil   pencils, penciled, penciling

pennant   pennants

penny   pennies, penniless

people   peoples, peopled, peopling

percent   percents, percentage, percentages, percentile, percentiles

perfect   perfects, perfected, perfecting, perfectly, perfectness, perfection, perfectionist

perform   performs, performed, performing, performance, performances, performer, performers

perfume   perfumes, perfumed, perfumer, perfumers, perfumery, perfumeries

perhaps

peril   perils, periled, periling, perilous, perilously

period   periods, periodical, periodicals, periodically

perish   perishes, perished, perishing, perishable, perishables

permanent   permanently, permanence, permanency

permit   permits, permitted, permitting, permission, permissions, permissible, permissive, permissively, permissiveness

persevere   perseveres, persevered, persevering, perseverance

persist   persists, persisted, persisting, persistent, persistently, persistence, persistency

person   persons, personal, personally, personable, personalize, personality, personalities

persuade   persuades, persuaded, persuading, persuasive, persuasively, persuasiveness, persuasion, persuasions, persuader, persuaders

pet pets

petition   petitions, petitioned, petitioning, petitioner, petitioners

petrify   petrifies, petrified, petrifying, petrification

phone phones, phoned, phoning

photograph photographs, photographed, photographing, photo, photography, photographer, photographers

phrase phrases, phrased, phrasing

physical physically

physician physicians

physics physicist, physicists

piano pianos, pianist, pianists

pick picks, picked, picking, picky, picker, pickers

pickle pickles, pickled, pickling

picnic picnics, picnicked, picnicking, picnicker, picnickers

picture pictures, pictured, picturing

pie pies

piece pieces, pieced, piecing

pier piers

pierce pierces, pierced, piercing, piercingly

pig pigs, piglet, piglets

pigeon pigeons

pile piles, piled, piling

pilgrim pilgrims, pilgrimage, pilgrimages

pillow pillows, pillowed, pillowing

pin pins, pinned, pinning

pink pinker, pinkest

pitch pitches, pitched, pitching, pitcher, pitchers

pity   pities, pitied, pitying, pityingly, pitiful, pitifully, piteous, piteously

pivot   pivots, pivoted, pivoting, pivotal, pivotally

place   places, placed, placing, placement, placements

plain   plains, plainer, plainest, plainly, plainness

plan   plans, planned, planning, planner, planners

plane   planes, planed, planing

planet   planets, planetary, planetarium, planetariums

plank   planks, planked, planking

plant   plants, planted, planting, planter, planters, plantation, plantations

plaster   plasters, plastered, plastering, plasterer, plasterers

plastic   plastics

platform   platforms

play   plays, played, playing, playful, playfully, playfulness, player, players

playground   playgrounds

playmate   playmates

pleasant   pleasantly, pleasantness, pleasantry, pleasantries, pleasance

please   pleases, pleased, pleasing, pleasingly, pleaser, pleasers

pleasure pleasures, pleasured, pleasuring, pleasurable, pleasurably, pleasureful, pleasurefully

pledge pledges, pledged, pledging, pledgee, pledgees

plenty plentiful, plentifully, plentifulness

plum plums

plunge plunges, plunged, plunging, plunger, plungers

pocket pockets, pocketed, pocketing, pocketful, pocketfuls

pocketbook pocketbooks

poem poems, poet, poets, poetry, poetries

point points, pointed, pointing, pointedly, pointless, pointer, pointers

poise poises, poised, poising

poison poisons, poisoned, poisoning, poisonous

police

policy policies

polish polishes, polished, polishing, polisher, polishers

polite politely, politeness

politics politic, politick, politicking, political, politically, politicize, politician, politicians

pollute pollutes, polluted, polluting, pollution, pollutant, pollutants, polluter

pond ponds

pony   ponies

pool   pools

poor   poorer, poorest, poorly, poorness

popcorn

popular   popularly, popularity, popularize, popularizes

porch   porches

porter   porters

portion   portions, portioned, portioning

pose   posed, posing, posable

position   positions, positioned, positioning

positive   positively, positiveness

possess   possesses, possessed, possessing, possession, possessions, possessive, possessively, possessiveness, possessor, possessors

possible   possibly, possibility, possibilities

post   posts, posted, posting, postage, postal

poster   posters

postpone   postpones, postponed, postponing, postponement, postponements

pot   pots, potted, potting

potato   potatoes

potential   potentially, potentiality

poultry   poultries

pound   pounds, pounded, pounding, poundage, poundages, lb., lbs.

pour pours, poured, pouring, pourable

poverty poverties

powder powders, powdered, powdering

power powers, powered, powering, powerful, powerfully, powerfulness, powerless, powerlessly, powerlessness

practice practices, practiced, practicing, practical, practically, practicality, practicalness, practicable, practitioner, practitioners

prairie prairies

praise praises, praised, praising

preach preaches, preached, preaching, preacher, preachers

precaution precautions, precautionary

precious preciously, preciousness

precise precisely, preciseness, precision, precisionist, precisionists

predict predicts, predicted, predicting, predictable

prefer prefers, preferred, preferring, preferable, preferably, preferential, preference, preferences

preliminary preliminaries, preliminarily

premature prematurely

premium premiums

prepare prepares, prepared, preparing, preparedly, preparatory, preparedness, preparation, preparations

present presents, presented, presenting, presentable, presently, presentably, presentation, presentations, presenter, presenters, presence

preside presides, presided, presiding, presider, presiders

president presidents, presidential, presidency

press presses, pressed, pressing, pressingly

pressure pressures, pressured, pressuring, pressurize, pressurizes, pressurized, pressurizing

presume presumes, presumed, presuming, presumedly, presumptive, presumptous, presumption, presumptions, presumably

pretend pretends, pretended, pretending, pretender, pretenders, pretentious, pretentiously

pretty prettier, prettiest, prettily, prettiness

prevail prevails, prevailed, prevailing, prevailingly, prevailer, prevailers

prevent prevents, prevented, preventing, preventable, preventative, preventive, preventiveness, prevention, preventions

previous previously

price prices, priced, pricing, priceless, pricelessly

pride prides, prided, priding, prideful, pridefully

prim   prims, primmed, primming, primmer, primmest, primly, primness

primary   primaries, primarily

prime   primes, primed, priming, primely, primer, primers

primitive   primitives, primitively, primitivism

prince   princes, princely, princess, princesses

principal   principals, principality

principle   principles, principled

print   prints, printed, printing, printer, printers

prior   priority, priorities

prison   prisons, prisoner, prisoners

private   privates, privately, privacy

privilege   privileges, privileged

prize   prizes, prized, prizing

probably   probable, probability, probabilities

problem   problems, problematic, problematically

procedure   procedures, procedural, procedurally

proceed   proceeds, proceeded, proceeding, proceedingly

process   processes, processed, processing

procession   processions, processional, processionals

proclaim proclaims, proclaimed, proclaiming, proclamation, proclamations

produce produces, produced, producing, producer, producers, producible

product products, productive, productively, productiveness, productivity, production, productions

profess professes, professed, professing, profession, professions, professional, professionally, professionalism, professor, professors

profit profits, profited, profiting, profitable, profitably, profitability, profitabilities

program programs, programmed, programming, programmer, programmers

progress progresses, progressed, progressing, progressive, progressively, progression, progressions

project projects, projected, projecting, projector, projectors

prominent prominently, prominence, prominences

promise promises, promised, promising, promisingly, promissory, promissories

promote promotes, promoted, promoting, promotable, promotion, promotions, promotional, promoter, promoters

prompt prompts, prompted, prompting, promptly, promptness, prompter, prompters

pronounce pronounces, pronounced, pronouncing, pronounceable, pronounceability, pronunciation, pronunciations, pronouncement, pronouncements

proper properly, properness

propose proposes, proposed, proposing, proposal, proposals

propriety proprieties

prosper prospers, prospered, prospering, prosperity, prosperous, prosperously

protect protects, protected, protecting, protection, protections, protective, protector, protectors

protest protests, protested, protesting, protester, protesters, protestation, protestations

proud prouder, proudest, proudly

prove proves, proved, proof, proofs, proofed, proofing, proven, proving

provide provides, provided, providing, provider, providers, provision, provisions

provoke provokes, provoked, provoking, provocative, provocatively, provocation, provocations, provoker, provokers

prune prunes, pruned, pruning

psychology psychologies, psychologize, psychological, psychologically, psychologist, psychologists

public   publics, publicly, publicize, publicizes, publicized, publicizing, publicity, publicist, publicists

publish   publishes, published, publishing, publisher, publishers, publication, publications

pull   pulls, pulled, pulling

pump   pumps, pumped, pumping, pumper, pumpers

pumpkin   pumpkins

punctual   punctually, punctualness, punctuality

punish   punishes, punished, punishing, punishable, punishment, punishments

puny   punier, puniest, puniness

pupil   pupils

puppy   puppies, puppyish, puppyishly

purchase   purchases, purchased, purchasing, purchasable

purple   purples, purpled, purpling, purplish

purpose   purposes, purposely, purposeful, purposefully, purposefulness, purposeless

purse   purses, pursed, pursing

pursue   pursues, pursued, pursuing, pursuance, pursuances, pursuer, pursuers, pursuit, pursuits

push   pushes, pushed, pushing, pushiness, pushy

put   puts, putting

puzzle   puzzles, puzzled, puzzling, puzzler, puzzlers, puzzlement, puzzlements

Q

quaint quainter, quaintest, quaintly, quaintness

qualify qualifies, qualified, qualifying, qualification, qualifications, qualifier, qualifiers

quality qualities

quantify quantifies, quantified, quantifying

quantity quantities, quantitative, quantitatively

quarrel quarrels, quarreled, quarreling, quarrelsome, quarreler, quarrelers

quart quarts

quarter quarters, quartered, quartering, quarterly

queen queens, queenly, queenlier, queenliest

quest quests, quested, questing

question questions, questioned, questioning, questionable, questionably, questioner, questioners, questionnaire, questionnaires

quick quicker, quickest, quickly, quickness

quiet quiets, quieted, quieting, quieter, quietest, quietly, quietness

quit quits, quitted, quitting, quitter, quitters

quite

quote quotes, quoted, quoting, quotable, quotation, quotations, quoter, quoters

R

rabbit   rabbits

race   races, raced, racing, racer, racers

rack   racks

racket   rackets, racketeers, racketeering

radiant   radiantly, radiate, radiates, radiated, radiating, radiance, radiation, radiator, radiators

radio   radios

rag   rags, ragged, raggedly, raggedness

raid   raids, raided, raiding, raider, raiders

rain   rains, rained, raining, rainy, rainier, rainiest

raise   raises, raised, raising

raisin   raisins

rake   rakes, raked, raking

rally   rallies, rallied, rallying

ranch   ranches, ranching, rancher, ranchers

random   randomly, randomness

range   ranges, ranged, ranging, ranger, rangers

rank   ranks, ranked, ranking

rapid   rapids, rapidly, rapidity, rapidness

rare   rarer, rarest, rarely, rareness, rarity, rarities

rascal   rascals, rascally

rat rats

rate rates, rated, rating, ratings, ratio, ratios, ration, rations

rather

ray rays

reach reaches, reached, reaching, reachable

read reads, reading, readable, reader, readers

ready readier, readiest, readiness

real realism, realist, realistic, reality, realities

realize realizes, realized, realizing, realization, realizations

really

reason reasons, reasoned, reasoning, reasonable, reasonably, reasonableness

receive receives, received, receiving, receipt, receipts, receivable, receiver, receivers, reception, receptive

recent recently, recentness, recency

recess recesses, recessed, recessing, recession, recessions

reckless recklessly, recklessness

recognize recognizes, recognized, recognizing, recognizable, recognition

recommend recommends, recommended, recommending, recommendable, recommendation, recommendations

record records, recorded, recording, recorder, recorders

recover   recovers, recovered, recovering, recovery, recoveries

red   redden, reddened, reddening, redder, reddest

reduce   reduces, reduced, reducing, reducible, reduction, reductions

refer   refers, referred, referring, reference, references, referenced, referencing, referral, referrals

refine   refines, refined, refining, refiner, refiners, refinement, refinements, refinery, refineries

reflect   reflects, reflected, reflection, reflections, reflector, reflectors

reflex   reflexes, reflexed, reflexing, reflexive, reflexively

reform   reforms, reformed, reforming, reformation, reformatory, reformatories, reformer, reformers

refrigerate   refrigerates, refrigerated, refrigerating, refrigeration, refrigerator, refrigerators

refuge   refuges, refuged, refuging, refugee, refugees

refuse   refuses, refused, refusing, refusal, refusals

regain   regains, regained, regaining

regard   regards, regarded, regarding, regardless, regardlessly

register   registers, registered, registering, registration, registrations, registrant, registrants, registry, registrar, registrars

regret   regrets, regretted, regretting, regretful, regretfully, regrettable

regular   regularly, regularity, regulate, regulates, regulated, regulating, regulation, regulations

reign   reigns, reigned, reigning

reinforce   reinforces, reinforced, reinforcing, reinforcement, reinforcements

reject   rejects, rejected, rejecting, rejection, rejections

relate   relates, related, relating, relation, relations, relative, relatives, relatively

relax   relaxes, relaxed, relaxing, relaxant, relaxants, relaxation

release   releases, released, releasing

relieve   relieves, relieved, relieving, relievable, reliever, relievers, relief, reliefs

religion   religions, religious, religiously, religiousness

rely   relies, relied, relying, reliable, reliably, reliability

remain   remains, remained, remaining, remainder, remainders

remark   remarks, remarked, remarking, remarkable, remarkably

remedy   remedies, remedied, remedying

remember   remembers, remembered, remembering, remembrance, remembrances

remind   reminds, reminded, reminding, reminder, reminders

remnant   remnants

remote   remoter, remotest, remotely, remoteness

remove   removes, removed, removing, remover, removers, removal, removable

render   renders, rendered, rendering, rendition, renditions

renew   renews, renewed, renewing, renewable, renewal, renewals

rent   rents, rented, renting, rental, rentals, renter, renters

repair   repairs, repaired, repairing, repairer, repairers

repeat   repeats, repeated, repeating, repeatable, repeatedly, repetitious, repetitiously, repetitive, repetitively, repetition, repetitions, repeater, repeaters

replace   replaces, replaced, replacing, replacement, replacements

reply   replies, replied, replying

report   reports, reported, reporting, reporter, reporters

represent   represents, represented, representing, representable, representation, representative, representatives

republic   republics, republican, republicans

request   requests, requested, requesting

require   requires, required, requiring, requirement, requirements

research   researches, researched, researching, researcher, researchers

resemble   resembles, resembled, resembling, resemblance

resent   resents, resented, resenting, resentful, resentfully, resentment, resentments

reserve   reserves, reserved, reserving, reservedly, reservation, reservations

reside   resides, resided, residing, residence, residences, residency, residencies, resident, residential

resist   resists, resisted, resisting, resistance, resistant, resistible, resister, resisters

resolve   resolves, resolved, resolving, resolvable, resolution, resolutions

resort   resorts, resorted, resorting

resource   resources, resourceful, resourcefully, resourcefulness

respect   respects, respected, respecting, respectable, respectably, respectability, respectful, respectfully

response   responses, responsible, responsibly, responsibility, responsibilities

rest   rests, rested, resting

restaurant   restaurants

restore   restores, restored, restoring, restorable, restoration, restorations

result   results, resulted, resulting

resume   resumes, resumed, resuming, resumption, resumptions

retain   retains, retained, retaining, retainable, retention, retainment, retainer, retainers

retreat   retreats, retreated, retreating

return   returns, returned, returning, returnable

reverse   reverses, reversed, reversing, reversely, reversal, reversals, reversible, reversibility, reversibilities

revise   revises, revised, revising, revision, revisions

revolt   revolts, revolted, revolting, revolution, revolutions, revolutionary, revolutionaries, revolutionist, revolutionize, revolutionized

revolve   revolves, revolved, revolving, revolvable, revolver, revolvers

reward   rewards, rewarded, rewarding

ribbon   ribbons

rice

rich   riches, richer, richest, richly, richness

ride   rides, rode, ridden, riding, rider, riders

ridicule   ridicules, ridiculed, ridiculing, ridiculous, ridiculously, ridiculousness

rifle   rifles, rifled, rifling, riflery

right   rights, righted, rightly, rightness

rigid   rigidly, rigidity, rigidness

ring   rings, rang rung, ringing

rinse   rinses, rinsed, rinsing

ripe   riper, ripest, ripen, ripens, ripened, ripening, ripeness

rise   rises, risen, rising

risk   risks, risked, risking, riskier, riskiest, risky

rival   rivals, rivaled, rivaling, rivalry, rivalries

river   rivers

road   roads

roam   roams, roamed, roaming

roar   roars, roared, roaring

robin   robins

robot   robots, robotic, robotics

rock   rocks, rocked, rocking, rocky, rockier, rockiest

roll   rolls, rolled, rolling, roller, rollers

roof   roofs, roofed, roofing, roofer, roofers

room   rooms, roomy, roomier, roomiest

rooster   roosters

root   roots, rooted, rooting

rope   ropes, roped, roping

rose   roses, rosy

rot   rots, rotted, rotting, rotten, rottener, rottenest, rottenly, rottenness

rotate   rotates, rotated, rotating, rotation, rotations, rotational, rotator, rotators, rotary, rotaries

rough   roughs, roughed, roughing, rougher, roughest, roughly, roughness

round   rounder, roundest, roundly

route   routes, routed, routing

row   rows, rowed, rowing, rower, rowers

rubber   rubbers, rubbery, rubberize, rubberizing

rudder   rudders

rude   ruder, rudest, rudely, rudeness

ruin   ruins, ruined, ruining, ruinous, ruinously

rule   rules, ruled, ruling, rulings, ruler, rulers

run   runs, ran, running, runner, runners

runaway   runaways

rural   rurally

rush   rushes, rushed, rushing

rustle   rustles, rustled, rustling, rustler, rustlers

ruth   ruthless, ruthlessly, ruthlessness

S

sack   sacks, sacked, sacking

sacrifice   sacrifices, sacrificed,
   sacrificing, sacrificial

sad   sadder, saddest, sadden, sadly, sadness

saddle   saddles, saddled, saddling

safe   safes, safer, safest, safely, safeness,
   safety

sail   sails, sailed, sailing, sailor, sailors

salad   salads

salary   salaries, salaried

salesperson   salespeople

salt   salts, salted, salting, salty, saltier,
   saltiest

salute   salutes, saluted, saluting, salutation,
   salutations

same   sameness

sample   samples, sampled, sampling,
   sampler, samplers

sand   sandy, sandier, sandiest

sandwich   sandwiches, sandwiched,
   sandwiching

sanitary   sanitarily, sanitation, sanitize,
   sanitizes, sanitized, sanitizing

sarcasm   sarcastic, sarcastically

satellite   satellites

satisfy   satisfies, satisfied, satisfying, satisfyingly, satisfactory, satisfactorily, satisfaction

saturate   saturates, saturated, saturating, saturation

Saturday   Sat.

sauce   sauces, sauced, saucing, saucer, saucers, saucy

savage   savages, savagely, savageness

save   saves, saved, saving, savings, saver, savers

say   says, said, saying

scale   scales, scaled, scaling, scaly

scant   scanty, scantly, scantness, scantily

scar   scars, scarred, scarring

scarce   scarcer, scarcest, scarcely, scarceness, scarcity, scarcities

scare   scares, scared, scaring, scary, scarier, scariest, scariness

scarf   scarves

scatter   scatters, scattered, scattering

scene   scenes, scenic, scenery, scenario, scenarios

scent   scents, scented, scenting

schedule   schedules, scheduled, scheduling, scheduler, schedulers

scheme   schemes, schemed, scheming, schemer, schemers, schematic, schematics

scholar   scholars, scholarly, scholarship, scholarships, scholastic, scholastics, scholastically

school   schools

schoolmate   schoolmates

science   sciences, scientist, scientists, scientific, scientifically

scissors

scold   scolds, scolded, scolding

score   scores, scored, scoring, scorer, scorers

scorn   scorns, scorned, scorning, scornful, scornfully, scornfulness

scowl   scowls, scowled, scowling

scramble   scrambles, scrambled, scrambling, scrambler, scramblers

scrap   scraps, scrapped, scrapping, scrapper, scrappers, scrappy, scrappier, scrappiest

scrape   scrapes, scraped, scraping, scraper, scrapers

scratch   scratches, scratched, scratching, scratchy, scratchier, scratchiest, scratchiness, scratcher, scratchers

scream   screams, screamed, screaming, screamer, screamers

screwdriver   screwdrivers

scrub   scrubs, scrubbed, scrubbing, scrubber, scrubbers

sea   seas

seal   seals, sealed, sealing, sealer, sealers

search   searches, searched, searching, searchingly

seashore   seashores

season   seasons, seasoned, seasoning, seasonable, seasonal, seasonably, seasonally

seat   seats, seated, seating

seclude   secludes, secluded, secluding, seclusive, seclusion

second   seconds, seconded, seconding, secondly

secret   secrets, secretive, secretly, secrecy

secretary   secretaries, secretarial

section   sections, sectioned, sectioning, sectional, sectionally, sectionalize

secure   secures, secured, securing, securely, security, securities

see   sees, saw, seen, seeing

seed   seeds, seeded, seeding, seeder, seeders, seedling, seedlings

seem   seems, seemed, seeming, seemingly

segment   segments, segmented, segmenting, segmentary, segmental, segmentation, segmentations

segregate   segregates, segregated, segregating, segregative, segregation, segregationist, segregationists

seize   seizes, seized, seizing, seizure, seizures

seldom   seldomly

select   selects, selected, selecting, selective, selectively, selectness, selection, selections

self-centered   self-centeredly, self-centeredness

self-conscious   self-consciously, self-consciousness

selfish   selfishly, selfishness

selfless   selflessly, selflessness

sell   sells, sold, selling, seller, sellers

semester   semesters

senate   senates, senator, senators

send   sends, sent, sending, sender, senders

senior   seniors, seniority

sensation   sensations, sensational, sensationalize, sensationally

sense   senses, sensed, sensing, sensible, sensibly, sensibility, senseless, sensory

sensitive   sensitively, sensitivity, sensitivities

sentence   sentences, sentenced, sentencing

sentiment   sentiments, sentimental, sentimentally, sentimentalist, sentimentalists

separate   separates, separated, separating, separately, separation, separations, separateness, separable, separator, separators

September   Sept.

sequence   sequences, sequenced, sequencing, sequent, sequential, sequentially

serious   seriously, seriousness

serve   serves, served, serving, server, servers, servant, servants, service, services

session   sessions

set   sets, setting, settings

settle   settles, settled, settling, settler, settlers, settlement, settlements

seven   sevens, seventh, sevenths

several

severe   severer, severest, severely, severity, severeness

sew   sews, sewed, sewn, sewing

shack   shacks

shade   shades, shaded, shading, shadiness, shady, shadier, shadiest

shadow   shadows, shadowed, shadowing, shadowy

shaft   shafts

shake   shakes, shook, shaking, shaken, shaky, shakier, shakiest, shakily, shaker, shakers

shall

shame   shames, shamed, shaming, shameful, shamefully, shameless, shamelessly, shamelessness

shape   shapes, shaped, shaping, shapely, shapeless

share

share   shares, shared, sharing

shark   sharks

sharp   sharper, sharpest, sharply,
    sharpness, sharpen, sharpens, sharpened,
    sharpening

she   she's

shed   sheds, shedding, shedder, shedders

sheep   sheepish, sheepishly

sheer   sheerly, sheerness

sheet   sheets, sheeting

shell   shells, shelled, shelling

shelter   shelters, sheltered, sheltering

sheriff   sheriffs

shield   shields, shielded, shielding

shine   shines, shined, shone, shining, shiny,
    shinier, shiniest

ship   ships, shipped, shipping, shipment,
    shipments, shipper, shippers

shirt   shirts

shock   shocks, shocked, shocking,
    shockingly, shocker, shockers

shoe   shoes

shop   shops, shopped, shopping, shopper,
    shoppers

shore   shores

short   shorter, shortest, shortly, shorten,
    shortens, shortened, shortening,
    shortness

should shouldn't

shoulder shoulders, shouldered, shouldering

shout shouts, shouted, shouting

shovel shovels, shoveled, shoveling

show shows, showed, shown, showing, showy

shower showers, showered, showering

shut shuts, shutting, shutter, shutters

sick sicker, sickest, sickly, sicken, sickens, sickened, sickening, sickeningly, sickness, sicknesses

side sides, sided, siding

sidewalk sidewalks

sideways

sigh sighs, sighed, sighing

sight sights, sighted, sighting, sightless

sign signs, signed, signing, signer, signers

signal signals, signaled, signaling, signaler, signalers

signature signatures

signify signifies, signified, signifying, signifiable, significant, significantly, significance, significancy

silent silently, silence, silences, silenced, silencing, silencer, silencers

silk silks, silkier, silkiest, silky, silken

silly sillier, silliest, silliness

silver   silvers, silvered, silvery

similar   similarly, similarity, simile, similes

simple   simply, simpler, simplest, simplicity, simplify, simplifies, simplified, simplifying, simplifier, simplifiers

since

sincere   sincerely, sincerest, sincerity

sing   sings, sang, sung, singing, singer, singers

single   singles, singled, singling, singly, singular, singulars, singularity, singularly

sink   sinks, sank, sunk, sunken, sinking

sir   sirs

sister   sisters

sit   sits, sat, sitting, sitter, sitters

situate   situates, situated, situating, situation, situations

six   sixes, sixth, sixths

sixteen   sixteens, sixteenth

size   sizes, sized, sizing

skate   skates, skated, skating, skater, skaters

skeleton   skeletons, skeletal, skeletals

sketch   sketches, sketched, sketching, sketchy, sketcher, sketchers, sketchier, sketchiest, sketchily, sketchiness

ski   skis, skied, skiing, skier, skiers

skid   skids, skidded, skidding

skill   skills, skilled, skillful, skillfully, skillfulness

skim   skims, skimmed, skimming, skimmer, skimmers

skin   skins, skinned, skinning

skirt   skirts, skirted, skirting

skit   skits, skittish, skittishly

sky   skies

sled   sleds, sledding

sleep   sleeps, slept, sleeping, sleeper, sleepers, sleepy, sleepier, sleepiest, sleepily

sleeve   sleeves, sleeved, sleeveless

sleigh   sleighs, sleighed, sleighing

slice   slices, sliced, slicing, slicer, slicers

slide   slides, slid, sliding, slider, sliders

slight   slights, slighted, slighting, slighter, slightest, slightly, slightness

slip   slips, slipped, slipping, slippery, slipperier, slipperiest, slipperiness, slipper, slippers

slither   slithers, slithered, slithering, slithery .

slow   slows, slowed, slowing, slower, slowest, slowly, slowness

slumber   slumbers, slumbered, slumbering, slumberer, slumberers

small   smaller, smallest, smallness

smash   smashes, smashed, smashing,
smashingly

smear   smears, smeared, smearing

smell   smells, smelled, smelling, smelly,
smellier, smelliest

smile   smiles, smiled, smiling

smirk   smirks, smirked, smirking,
smirker

smoke   smokes, smoked, smoking, smoky,
smokier, smokiest, smoker, smokers

smolder   smolders, smoldered, smoldering

smooth   smooths, smoothed, smoothing,
smoother, smoothest, smoothly,
smoothness

smother   smothers, smothered, smothering

snag   snags, snagged, snagging

snake   snakes

snap   snaps, snapped, snapping, snapper,
snappers

sneak   sneaks, sneaked, sneaking, sneaky,
sneakier, sneakiest

sneaker   sneakers

sneeze   sneezes, sneezed, sneezing

snoop   snoops, snooped, snooping, snooper,
snoopers, snoopy, snoopier, snoopiest

snow   snows, snowed, snowing, snowy,
snowier, snowiest

snowball   snowballs, snowballed, snowballing

so

so-called

soak   soaks, soaked, soaking

soap   soaps, soaped, soaping, soapy, soapier, soapiest

sob   sobs, sobbed, sobbing

social   socials, socially, sociable, sociably, sociableness, society, societies, societal, socialize, socializes, socialized, socializing, socialism, socialist, socialists, socialization, sociability

sock   socks, socked, socking

soft   soften, softer, softest, softly, softness

soil   soils, soiled, soiling

sole   soles, soled, soling

solemn   solemnly, solemnize, solemnify, solemnity, solemnness

solid   solids, solidity, solidify, solidifies, solidified, solidifying, solidifier, solidifiers, solidarity, solidarities

solitary   solitarily, solitude

solo   solos, soloing, soloed, soloist, soloists

solution   solutions

solve   solves, solved, solving, solvable, solver, solvers

some   somebody, somehow, someone, something, sometimes, somewhat, somewhere

somersault somersaults, somersaulted, somersaulting

son sons

song songs, songster, songsters

soon sooner, soonest

sore sores, sorer, sorest, sorely, soreness

sorrow sorrows, sorrowed, sorrowing, sorrowful, sorrowfully, sorrowfulness

sorry sorrier, sorriest, sorrily

sort sorts, sorted, sorting, sorter, sorters

sound sounds, sounded, sounding, sounder, soundest

sour sours, soured, sourest, souring, sourly, sourness

source sources

south southward, southerly, southern, southerner, southerners

space spaces, spaced, spacing, spacer, spacers, spacious, spaciously, spaciousness

spade spades, spaded, spading

spare spares, spared, sparing, sparingly, spareness

sparkle sparkles, sparkled, sparkling, sparkler, sparklers

sparrow sparrows

speak speaks, spoke, spoken, speaking, speaker, speakers

special specials, specialize, specializes, specialized, specializing, specialization, specialty, specialties, specialist, specialists

species

specify specifies, specified, specifying, specific, specifics, specifically, specification, specifications, specificity, specificities, specifier, specifiers

specimen specimens

speech speeches, speechless, speechlessness

speed speeds, speeded, sped, speeding, speedy, speedier, speediest, speedily, speeder, speeders

spell spells, spelled, spelling, speller, spellers

spend spends, spent, spending, spendable, spender, spenders

sphere spheres, sphered, spherical

spill spills, spilled, spilling, spillage

spin spins, spun, spinning, spinner, spinners

spirit spirits, spirited, spiritual, spirituality, spiritless

spite spites, spited, spiting, spiteful, spitefully, spitefulness

splash splashes, splashed, splashing, splashy, splashier, splashiest, splasher, splashers

splendid splendidly, splendidness, splendor, splendors, splendorous, splendorously

split splits, splitting, splitter, splitters

spoil spoils, spoiled, spoiling, spoiler, spoilers

spoon spoons, spooned, spooning, spooner, spooners

sport sports, sported, sporting

spot spots, spotted, spotting, spotter, spotters

sprawl sprawls, sprawled, sprawling

spray sprays, sprayed, spraying, sprayer, sprayers

spread spreads, spreading, spreader, spreaders

spring springs, sprang, sprung, springing, springy, springier, springiest, springiness

sprinkle sprinkles, sprinkled, sprinkling, sprinkler, sprinklers

spry spryly, sprier, spriest, spryness

squall squalls, squalled, squalling

square squares, squared, squaring, squarest, squarish, squarely, squareness

squash squashes, squashed, squashing, squashy, squashier, squashiest, squashiness

squeeze squeezes, squeezed, squeezing, squeezable, squeezer, squeezers

squirrel   squirrels, squirreled, squirreling

stable   stables, stabled, stabling, stabler,
  stablest, stability

stack   stacks, stacked, stacking

staff   staffs, staffed, staffing

stair   stairs

stairway   stairways, stairwell, stairwells

stake   stakes, staked, staking

stalk   stalks, stalked, stalking, stalker,
  stalkers

stamp   stamps, stamped, stamping, stamper,
  stampers

stand   stands, stood, standing

standard   standards, standardize,
  standardized

star   stars

stare   stares, stared, staring, staringly,
  starer, starers

start   starts, started, starting, starter,
  starters

startle   startles, startled, startling

starve   starves, starved, starving,
  starvation

state   states, stated, stating, stately,
  statelier, stateliest

station   stations, stationed, stationing,
  stationary

stationery

statue statues, statuette, statuettes, statuary

stay stays, stayed, staying

steady steadies, steadied, steadying, steadier, steadiest, steadily, steadiness

steal steals, stole, stolen, stealing, stealer, stealers

steam steams, steamed, steaming, steamer, steamers, steamy, steamier, steamiest

steel steels, steely, steelier, steeliest

steep steeper, steepest, steeply

steer steers, steered, steering, steerable, steerer, steerers, steerage

step steps, stepped, stepping

sterile sterility, sterilize, sterilizes, sterilized, sterilizing, sterilization

stick sticks, stuck, sticking, sticky, stickier, stickiest, stickiness

still stillness

stimulate stimulates, stimulated, stimulating, stimulative, stimulation, stimulus, stimulant, stimulants, stimulator, stimulators

sting stings, stung, stinging, stinger, stingers

stingy stingier, stingiest, stingily, stinginess

stir stirs, stirred, stirring, stirrer, stirrers

stitch   stitches, stitched, stitching, stitcher, stitchers

stocking   stockings

stomach   stomachs, stomached, stomaching

stone   stones, stoned, stoning

stoop   stoops, stooped, stooping

stop   stops, stopped, stopping, stopper, stoppers

store   stores, stored, storing

storm   storms, stormed, storming, stormy, stormier, stormiest

story   stories, storied

stove   stoves

straight   straighter, straightest, straightly, straightness, straighten, straightens, straightened, straightening, straightener, straighteners

strain   strains, strained, straining, strainer, strainers

strange   strangely, stranger, strangest, strangeness, strangers

strategy   strategies, strategic, strategically, strategist, strategists, stratagem

straw   straws

stray   strays, strayed, straying

stream   streams, streamed, streaming, streamer, streamers

street   streets

strength strengths, strengthen, strengthens, strengthened, strengthening, strengthener, strengtheners

strenuous strenuously, strenuousness

stretch stretches, stretched, stretching, stretchable, stretchy, stretchier, stretchiest, stretchiness, stretcher, stretchers

strict stricter, strictest, strictly, strictness

strike strikes, struck, striking, strikingly, striker, strikers

string strings, strung, stringing, stringy, stringier, stringiest

strip strips, stripped, stripping, stripper, strippers

stroll strolls, strolled, strolling, stroller, strollers

strong stronger, strongest, strongly

struggle struggles, struggled, struggling, struggler, strugglers

stubborn stubborner, stubbornest, stubbornly, stubbornness

student students

study studies, studied, studying, studious, studiously, studiousness

stuff stuffs, stuffed, stuffing, stuffy, stuffier, stuffiest

stump stumps, stumped, stumping, stumpy, stumpier, stumpiest

stupid stupider, stupidest, stupidity, stupidly

style styles, styled, styling, stylish, stylishly, stylishness, stylist, stylists

subject subjects, subjected, subjecting, subjective, subjectively

submarine submarines

submerge submerges, submerged, submerging, submergence

submit submits, submitted, submitting, submittance

subscribe subscribes, subscribed, subscribing, subscriber, subscribers, subscription, subscriptions

substance substances, substantial, substantially, substantiate, substantiates, substantiated, substantiating, substantive, substantiation

substitute substitutes, substituted, substituting, substitutable, substitution, substitutions, substitutional

suburb suburbs, suburban, suburbanite, suburbanites, suburbia

succeed succeeds, succeeded, succeeding

success successful, successfully, successfulness, succession, successive, successor, successors

such

sudden suddenly, suddenness

suffer suffers, suffered, suffering, sufferer, sufferers, sufferance

suffice   suffices, sufficed, sufficing, sufficient, sufficiency, sufficiently

suggest   suggests, suggested, suggesting, suggestible, suggestive, suggestively, suggestion, suggestions

suit   suits, suited, suiting, suitable, suitably, suitability

suite   suites

sulk   sulks, sulked, sulking, sulker, sulkers, sulky, sulkier, sulkiest, sulkily, sulkiness

sullen   sullenly, sullenness

sultry   sultrier, sultriest, sultriness

sum   sums, summed, summing

summary   summaries, summarized, summarizes, summarizing

summer   summers, summery

summons   summonses, summoned, summoning, summoner, summoners

sun   suns, sunned, sunning, sunny, sunnier, sunniest, sunniness

Sunday   Sun.

superb   superbly, superbness

superior   superiors, superiority

supervise   supervises, supervised, supervising, supervision, supervisor, supervisors, supervisory

supper   suppers

supplement   supplements, supplemented, supplementing, supplemental, supplementary, supplementation

supply   supplies, supplied, supplying, supplier, suppliers

support   supports, supported, supporting, supportable, supportive, supportively, supporter, supporters

suppose   supposes, supposed, supposing, supposedly, supposition, suppositions

supreme   supremely, supremacy, supremeness

sure   surely, surer, surest, sureness

surface   surfaces, surfaced, surfacing

surgeon   surgeons

surplus

surprise   surprises, surprised, surprising, surprisingly

surrender   surrenders, surrendered, surrendering

surround   surrounds, surrounded, surrounding, surroundings

survey   surveys, surveyed, surveying, surveyor, surveyors

suspect   suspects, suspected, suspecting, suspicion, suspicions, suspicious, suspiciously, suspiciousness

suspend   suspends, suspended, suspending, suspense, suspension, suspensions, suspenders

swallow   swallows, swallowed, swallowing

sway sways, swayed, swaying, swayer, swayers

sweater sweaters

sweep sweeps, swept, sweeping, sweeper, sweepers

sweet sweets, sweeter, sweetest, sweetly, sweeten, sweetness

swell swells, swelled, swelling, swollen, swollenly

swift swifter, swiftest, swiftly, swiftness

swim swims, swam, swum, swimming, swimmer, swimmers, swimmingly

swing swings, swung, swinging, swinger, swingers

switch switches, switched, switching, switcher, switchers

swivel swivels, swiveled, swiveling

sword swords

syllable syllables, syllabic, syllabicate, syllabication

symbol symbols, symbolic, symbolically, symbolism, symbolize, symbolizes, symbolized, symbolizing

sympathy sympathies, sympathize, sympathizes, sympathized, sympathizing, sympathizer, sympathetic, sympathetically

system systems, systematic, systematize, systematized, systematizing, systemic

T

table   tables, tabled, tabling

tablet   tablets

tackle   tackles, tackled, tackling, tackler, tacklers

tail   tails, tailed, tailing

tailor   tailors, tailored, tailoring

take   takes, took, taken, taking, taker, takers

talent   talents, talented

talk   talks, talked, talking, talkative, talker, talkers

tall   taller, tallest

tan   tans, tanned, tanning, tanner, tanners, tannest

tar   tars, tarred, tarring

tariff   tariffs

tarnish   tarnishes, tarnished, tarnishing

taxi   taxis, taxied, taxiing

teach   teaches, taught, teaching, teachable, teacher, teachers

team   teams, teamed, teaming, teamster, teamsters

tear   tears, tore, torn, teared, tearing, tearful, tearfully

telecommunication   telecommunications

telegraph

telegraph telegraphs, telegraphed, telegraphing, telegraphic, telegrapher, telegraphy

telephone telephones, telephoned, telephoning

television televisions, televise, televises, televised, televising

tell tells, told, telling, teller, tellers

temper tempers, tempered, tempering, temperament, temperaments, temperamental, temperamentally

temperature temperatures, temperate, temperately

tempo tempos, tempi

temporary temporarily, temporariness

tempt tempts, tempted, tempting, temptable, temptation, temptations, tempter, tempters

ten tens, tenth

tend tends, tended, tending, tendency, tendencies, tender

tennis

tent tents

term terms, termed, terming

terrible terribly, terribleness

territory territories, territorial, territorialize, territorializes, territorialized

terror   terrors, terrorize, terrorizes, terrorized, terrorizing, terrorizer, terrorism, terrorist, terrorists

test   tests, tested, testing, tester, testers

textile   textiles

texture   textures, textured, textural, texturally

than

thank   thanks, thanked, thanking, thankful, thankfully, thankless, thanksgiving

the

theater   theaters, theatrical, theatrically, theatrics

theft   thefts

their   theirs

them   themselves

then

theory   theories, theorize, theorizes, theorized, theorizing, theorist, theorists

therapy   therapies, therapeutic, therapist, therapists

there

thermometer   thermometers

they   they're

thick   thicker, thickest, thickly, thickness

thief   thieves, thieved, thieving, thievery, thievish, thievishly

thin   thinner, thinness, thinnest, thinly, thins, thinned, thinning

thing

thing   things

think   thinks, thinking, thinker, thinkers

thirst   thirsts, thirsted, thirsting, thirsty, thirstier, thirstiest, thirstily, thirstiness

thirteen   thirteens, thirteenth

thirty   thirties, thirtieth

this   that, these, those

thorough   thoroughly, thoroughness

though

thought   thoughts, thoughtful, thoughtfully, thoughtfulness, thoughtless, thoughtlessly, thoughtlessness

thousand   thousands, thousandth

thread   threads, threaded, threading, threader, threaders

threat   threats, threaten, threatens, threatened, threatening, threateningly

three   threes, third, thirds

thrill   thrills, thrilled, thrilling, thrillingly, thriller, thrillers

throat   throats, throaty, throatier, throatiest, throatily

throne   thrones

through

throw   throws, threw, thrown, throwing, thrower, throwers

thrust   thrusts, thrust, thrusting, thruster, thrusters

thumb   thumbs, thumbed, thumbing

thunder   thunders, thundered, thundering, thundery, thunderous, thunderously

Thursday   Thurs.

ticket   tickets, ticketed, ticketing, ticketer, ticketers

tickle   tickles, tickled, tickling, ticklish, ticklishly, ticklishness, tickler, ticklers

tide   tides, tidal

tie   ties, tied, tying

tight   tights, tighten, tightens, tightened, tightening, tighter, tightest, tightly, tightness

tile   tiles, tiled, tiling, tiler, tilers

time   times, timed, timing, timer, timers

timetable   timetables

timid   timidly, timidity, timidness

tin   tins, tinned, tinning, tinny

tiny   tinier, tiniest

tire   tires, tired, tiring, tireless, tirelessly, tiresome, tiresomely, tiredness

to   too

today

toe   toes

together   togetherness

tolerate   tolerates, tolerated, tolerating, tolerant, tolerable, tolerably, tolerantly, tolerance, tolerances, toleration

tomato   tomatoes

ton   tons

tone   tones, toned, toning, toneless, toner,
   toners

tongue   tongues

tonight

tool   tools, tooled, tooling

tooth   teeth, toothy, toothier, toothiest,
   toothless

top   tops, topped, topping

topic   topics, topical, topically

torment   torments, tormented, tormenting,
   tormentor, tormentors

torrent   torrents, torrential, torrentially

torrid   torridly, torridness

toss   tosses, tossed, tossing

total   totals, totaled, totaling, totally,
   totality, totalize, totalizes, totalized,
   totalizing, totalization

touch   touches, touched, touching, touchy,
   touchier, touchiest, touchable

tough   tougher, toughest, toughly, toughen,
   toughens, toughened, toughening,
   toughness

tour   tours, toured, touring, tourist,
   tourists, tourism

tournament   tournaments, tourney,
   tourneys

toward   towards

towel   towels, toweled, toweling

tower   towers, towered, towering

town   towns

toy   toys, toyed, toying

trace   traces, traced, tracing, tracer, tracers

track   tracks, tracked, tracking, tracker, trackers

trade   trades, traded, trading, trader, traders

tradition   traditions, traditional, traditionally, traditionalism, traditionalist, traditionalists

traffic   trafficked, trafficking

tragedy   tragedies, tragic, tragical, tragically

trail   trails, trailed, trailing, trailer, trailers

train   trains, trained, training, trainers, trainers

transfer   transfers, transferred, transferring, transferable, transferability, transferal, transferals, transference

transmit   transmits, transmitted, transmitting, transmittable, transmitter, transmitters, transmission, transmissions

transport   transports, transported, transporting, transportable, transportability, transportation, transporter, transporters

trap   traps, trapped, trapping, trapper, trappers

trash   trashy, trashier, trashiest

travel   travels, traveled, traveling, traveler, travelers

treasure   treasures, treasured, treasuring, treasury, treasuries, treasurer, treasurers

treat   treats, treated, treating, treatable, treatment, treatments

treaty   treaties

tree   trees

tremendous   tremendously

trial   trials

tribe   tribes, tribal

tribute   tributes, tributary, tributaries

trick   tricks, tricked, tricking, tricky, trickier, trickiest, trickster, tricksters

trifle   trifles, trifled, trifling

trim   trims, trimmed, trimming, trimmer, trimmest, trimly, trimness

trip   trips, tripped, tripping

triumph   triumphs, triumphed, triumphing, triumphant, triumphantly

troop   troops, trooped, trooping, trooper, troopers

trophy   trophies

trouble   troubles, troubled, troubling, troublesome

trout   trout

truck   trucks, trucked, trucking, trucker, truckers

true   truer, truest, truly, trueness

trunk   trunks

trust   trusts, trusted, trusting, trustful, trustfully, trustless, trustiness

truth   truths, truthful, truthfully, truthfulness

try   tries, tried, trying

Tuesday   Tues.

turn   turns, turned, turning

turtle   turtles

twelve   twelves, twelfth

twenty   twenties, twentieth

twenty-five   twenty-fives, twenty-fifth

twig   twigs

twilight   twilights

twin   twins

twist   twists, twisted, twisting, twister, twisters

two   twos, twice

typewriter   typewriters, typewrite, typewrites, typewritten, typewriting

typical   typically

typify   typifies, typified, typifying

U

ugly uglier, ugliest, ugliness

umbrella umbrellas

umpire umpires, umpired, umpiring

unanimous unanimously, unanimity

unavoidable unavoidably

unaware unawares

uncertain uncertainly, uncertainty, uncertainties, uncertainness

unclaimed

uncle uncles

uncomfortable uncomfortably

uncommon uncommonly, uncommonness

unconscious unconsciously, unconsciousness

under

underdog underdogs

undergraduate undergraduates

undergrowth

underrate underrates, underrated, underrating

undertake undertakes, undertook, undertaken, undertaking, undertaker, undertakers

undisputed undisputedly

undoubted undoubtedly

uneasy uneasier, uneasiest, uneasily, uneasiness

uneventful uneventfully

unexpected unexpectedly, unexpectedness

unfortunate unfortunately

uniform uniforms, uniformed, uniformly

unify unifies, unified, unifying

unimaginable unimaginableness

union unions, unionize, unionizes, unionized, unionizing, unionizer, unionizers

unit units

unite unites, united, uniting, unity, unities

universe universes, universal, universally, universalize, universalized, universalizing

university universities

unjust unjustly, unjustness

unless

unlimited

unload unloads, unloaded, unloading

unlock unlocks, unlocked, unlocking

unnecessary unnecessarily

unoccupied

unpack unpacks, unpacked, unpacking

unpleasant unpleasantly, unpleasantness

unpredictable unpredictably

unruly unrulier, unruliest, unruliness

until

unusual unusually, unusualness

unwilling unwillingly, unwillingness

unwise unwisely

unworthy unworthier, unworthiest, unworthily, unworthiness

unyielding

up upper, upward, upwards

uphold upholds, upheld, upholding, upholder, upholders

upon

upright uprightly, uprightness

uprising uprisings

upstairs

urban urbanism, urbanite, urbanites

urge urges, urged, urging, urgent, urgently, urgency

us

use uses, used, using, useful, usefully, usefulness, usable, usage, usages, useless, uselessly, uselessness

usher ushers, ushered, ushering

usual usually, usualness

utilize utilizes, utilized, utilizing, utilization, utility, utilities

utter utters, uttered, uttering, utterance, utterable, utterly, utmost, uttermost

V

vacant vacantly, vacantness, vacancy, vacancies, vacate, vacates, vacated, vacating

vacation vacations, vacationer, vacationers

vacuum vacuums, vacuumed, vacuuming

vague vaguer, vaguest, vaguely, vagueness

vain vainly, vainness, vanity, vanities

valentine valentines

valley valleys

value values, valued, valuing, valuably, valueless, valuate, valuable, valuables, valuation

vanish vanishes, vanished, vanishing

vary varies, varied, varying, various, variously, variable, variety, varieties, variant, variation

vast vaster, vastest, vastly, vastness

vegetable vegetables

vegetate vegetates, vegetated, vegetating, vegetation, vegetarian, vegetarians

velvet velvets, velvety, velvetiness, velveteen

vengeance vengeful, vengefully

venture ventures, ventured, venturing, venturer, venturers, venturesome, venturesomely

verify   verifies, verified, verifying, verification, verifiable, verifier, verifiers

versus vs.

vertical   vertically, verticalness

very

vessel vessels

vice vices

vicinity   vicinities

vicious   viciously, viciousness

victim   victims, victimize, victimizes, victimized, victimizing

victory   victories, victorious, victoriously, victoriousness, victor, victors

view   views, viewed, viewing, viewer, viewers

viewpoint   viewpoints

vigor   vigorous, vigorously, vigorousness

village   villages, villager, villagers

violent   violently, violence

virtue   virtues, virtuous, virtuously

visible   visibly, visibility, visibilities, visibleness

visit   visits, visited, visiting, visitation, visitor, visitors

visual   visually

vital   vitally, vitalize, vitalizes, vitalized, vitalizing, vitality

vocation   vocations, vocational, vocationally

voice   voices, voiced, voicing, voiceless, voicelessness

volcano   volcanoes, volcanic, volcanically

volume   volumes, voluminous, voluminously

volunteer   volunteers, volunteered, volunteering, voluntary, voluntarily

vote   votes, voted, voting, voter, voters

vouch   vouches, vouched, vouching, voucher, vouchers

vow   vows, vowed, vowing

voyage   voyages, voyaged, voyaging, voyager, voyagers

vulgar   vulgarly, vulgarity, vulgarities

W

wade   wades, waded, wading

wager   wagers, wagered, wagering, wagerer, wagerers

waist   waists

wait   waits, waited, waiting, waiter, waiters, waitress, waitresses

wake   wakes, waked, woke, waking, waken, wakens, wakened, wakening

walk   walks, walked, walking, walker, walkers

wall   walls, walled

wander   wanders, wandered, wandering, wanderer, wanderers

want   wants, wanted, wanting, wantingly

warehouse   warehouses, warehoused, warehousing

warm   warms, warmed, warming, warmer, warmest, warmly, warmth

warrant   warrants, warranted, warranting, warrantable, warranty, warranties

was

wash   washes, washed, washing, washer, washers

waste   wastes, wasted, wasting, wasteful, wastefully

watch   watches, watched, watching, watcher, watchers

water   waters, watered, watering, watery

way ways

we we're, we've

weak weaker, weakest, weakly, weakness

wealth wealthy, wealthier, wealthiest,
wealthily, wealthiness

wear wears, wore, worn, wearing

weary wearies, wearied, wearying,
wearier, weariest, wearily, weariness

weather

weave weaves, weaved, weaving, wove,
woven, weaver, weavers

Wednesday Wed.

weed weeds, weeded, weeding, weedy,
weedier, weediest

week weeks, weekly, weekday, weekdays,
weekend, weekends

weigh weighs, weighed, weighing, weigher,
weight, weights, weighty, weightier,
weightiest, weightless, weightlessness

weird weirdest, weirdly, weirdness

welcome welcomes, welcomed, welcoming

welfare

well wells

went

were weren't

west western, westerner, westerners,
westerly, westward

wet wetter, wettest, wetness

whale

whale   whales, whaling, whaler, whalers

what

wheat

wheel   wheels, wheeled, wheeling

when

where

whether

which

while

whimper   whimpers, whimpered,
   whimpering

whip   whips, whipped, whipping

whirl   whirls, whirled, whirling,
   whirlingly

whisper   whispers, whispered, whispering,
   whisperer, whisperers

whistle   whistles, whistled, whistling,
   whistler, whistlers

white   whiter, whitest, whited, whiting

who   whom, whose, whoever, whomever

whole   wholes, wholesome, wholly

why

wicked   wickedly, wickedness

wide   wider, widest, wideness, widely, widen

width   widths

wild   wilder, wildest, wildly, wilds,
   wildness, wilderness

will   would, wouldn't

win   wins, won, winning, winner, winners

wind   winds, wound, winding, windy, windier, windiest

window   windows

wing   wings, winged, winging, wingless

winter   winters, wintered, wintering

wire   wires, wired, wiring

wise   wiser, wisest, wisely, wisdom

wish   wishes, wished, wishing, wisher, wishers

with   without

withdraw   withdraws, withdrew, withdrawn, withdrawing, withdrawal, withdrawals

wither   withers, withered, withering, witheringly

witness   witnesses, witnessed, witnessing

woman   women, womanly

won't   will not

wonder   wonders, wondered, wondering, wonderful, wonderfully, wondrous, wondrously

wood   woods, wooded, wooden, woody

wool   wools, woolen, woolens, wooly, woolier, wooliest

word   words, worded, wording, wordy, wordier, wordiest

work

work   works, worked, working, worker, workers

world   worlds, worldly

worry   worries, worried, worrying, worrier, worriers

worse   worst

worth   worthy, worthier, worthiest, worthiness, worthless, worthlessness

wrap   wraps, wrapped, wrapping, wrapper, wrappers

wreck   wrecks, wrecked, wrecking, wreckage, wrecker, wreckers

wrench   wrenches, wrenched, wrenching

wrestle   wrestles, wrestled, wrestling, wrestler, wrestlers

wrist   wrists

write   writes, wrote, written, writing, writer, writers

wrong   wrongs, wronged, wronging, wrongly

Y

yard yards, yardage, yardages

year years, yearly

yell yells, yelled, yelling, yeller, yellers

yellow yellows, yellowed, yellowing

yes

yesterday yesterdays

yet

yield yields, yielded, yielding, yieldingly

you your

young younger, youngest, youngster, youngsters

yourself yourselves

youth youths, youthful, youthfully, youthfulness

Z

zoo zoos